T0301711

The authors of *Management and Leadership of Non-Profit Organisations in Singapore* draw on their extensive experience as leaders, consultants and researchers, to illuminate aspects of the management challenges faced by non-profit organisations in Singapore. The publication is timely. Although non-profits are not new to the social service ecosystem, there is room for more sharing of relevant lessons within and beyond the sector. This book is a helpful toolkit for non-profit leaders, to better equip ourselves and our teams for a dynamic future and, ultimately, to increase the impact of our mission.

Alicia Altorfer-Ong, Ph.D.
Partnership Director of crowdfunding charity Ray of Hope

This seminal work by Dr Caroline Lim, Dr Millie Su and Mr Sng Hock Lin shines timely and vital light on the non-profit sector in Singapore, allowing its readers much needed insights specifically from an Asian context. *Management and Leadership of Non-Profit Organisations in Singapore* is an important resource not only for executives and managers in charitable organisations and public institutions, but also for those in the for-profit sector championing corporate social responsibility, community and sustainability initiatives. By examining strategic blueprints and relevant, practicable frameworks, the book serves to cross-fertilise critical ideas and concepts across industry sectors and functions for organisations striving for its purpose-driven mission, and to inspire across generations for individuals seeking to create transformative social impact.

Anne Kim So Min
Former Board Member of Tsao Foundation,
Healthcare Private Equity & Venture Capital
investor and Founder of edutech Academy Pret

It is a delight to read such a book written by three NPO experts with such richly diverse work cultures and experiences. From the lenses of their individual thoughtful perspectives, the book represents how our local non-profit ecosystem can benefit from collaboration and co-creation by different stakeholders like themselves from across society. By offering clear definitions of commonly used and yet subjectively understood NPO terminology coupled with relevant management frameworks, the book invites fresh dialogue amongst practitioners through a common language to break down communication barriers for industry best practice. Be inspired by the summary bold vision of collective societal stewardship of Singapore's vital NPO sector.

Christina Cheng
Singapore Director of Theory of Constraints for Education
(TOCfE), Rotary Peace Fellow

This book invites the reader to reflect on many useful concepts contributing to the ingredients of success and effectiveness in the non-profit space. Peppered with numerous real examples graciously shared by fellow non-profit leaders, it leads us to contextualise non-profit management speak within our uniquely Singapore ecosystem. The chapters give the flavour of a business-school non-profit course, but are more than a series of case studies. Practical every-day perspectives are offered and readers are also invited by the authors to be in solidarity with them, to actively co-create a dynamic community of life-long learning. It is a compelling book that not only seeks to educate, but also advocates for one's personal growth and the sector's development.

Dr Christopher Lien
Geriatrician, Changi General Hospital
Governor, Lien Foundation

This book is timely for non-profit leaders to refresh their perspectives in understanding Singapore's non-profit climate. They can familiarise themselves with the new dynamics that may shape their organisations, and be intentional in driving sustainable "social" performances in the post-pandemic era. With broad topics covered using academic research aided by frameworks and models, and with references to local social service agencies, non-profit leaders can aspire to review, rethink and rejuvenate their organisations' strategic thrusts through thoughtful ideas shared in the seven chapters. New leaders entering the field can also be empowered to better navigate this volatile sector.

Dr Danny Tan
CEO of Odyssey Dance Theatre Ltd

MANAGEMENT AND LEADERSHIP OF NON-PROFIT ORGANISATIONS IN SINGAPORE

A Common Language and Shared
Meaning for Transformation

MANAGEMENT AND LEADERSHIP OF NON-PROFIT ORGANISATIONS IN SINGAPORE

A Common Language and Shared
Meaning for Transformation

Caroline S. L. Lim
Millie Yun Su
Hock Lin Sng

Singapore University of Social Sciences, Singapore

EW JERSEY · LONDON · SINGAPORE · BEIJING · SHANGHAI · HONG KONG · TAIPEI · CHENNAI · TOKYO

Published by

World Scientific Publishing Co. Pte. Ltd.
5 Toh Tuck Link, Singapore 596224
USA office: 27 Warren Street, Suite 401-402, Hackensack, NJ 07601
UK office: 57 Shelton Street, Covent Garden, London WC2H 9HE

Library of Congress Cataloging-in-Publication Data
Names: Lim, Caroline, author. | Su, Millie Yun, author. | Sng, Hock Lin, author.
Title: Management and leadership of non-profit organisations in Singapore : a common language
    and shared meaning for transformation / Caroline Lim, Millie Yun Su, Hock Lin Sng.
Description: New Jersey : World Scientific, [2022] | Includes bibliographical references and index.
Identifiers: LCCN 2022009720 | ISBN 9789811251498 (hardcover) |
    ISBN 9789811251504 (ebook) | ISBN 9789811251511 (ebook other)
Subjects: LCSH: Nonprofit organizations--Singapore--Management. |
    Organizational change--Singapore.
Classification: LCC HD62.6 .L55 2022 | DDC 361.7/63095957--dc23/eng/20220316
LC record available at https://lccn.loc.gov/2022009720

British Library Cataloguing-in-Publication Data
A catalogue record for this book is available from the British Library.

For any available supplementary material, please visit
https://www.worldscientific.com/worldscibooks/10.1142/12702#t=suppl

Desk Editor: Jiang Yulin

Typeset by Stallion Press
Email: enquiries@stallionpress.com

Printed in Singapore

*Song inspired by this book and composed by Cameron J. Tan,
co-written by Ang Wei Lun*

A Single Seed
The world is changing
Dividing us in half
Why are we against each other?

Your strength is waning
Will it ever be enough?
And how do we keep holding on?

But there's hope inside
If you shine a light

Chorus:
A single seed could grow into a forest
A single bulb could make it bright
A single voice becomes a chorus
A single hand could change a life

The future's daunting
The dream's so hard to chase
It doesn't have to be that way

You may seem weary
But there is power in your voice
Call for your brothers and sisters

There's hope inside
You've shone the light

Scan this to listen to the song

About the Authors

Caroline S. L. Lim is a practitioner-turned-academic at the Singapore University of Social Sciences (SUSS). She spent more than a decade in banking and finance before moving into higher education and public healthcare. Caroline received her PhD in Business from the Singapore Management University.

At SUSS, Caroline heads the Organisation and Leadership for Social Change programme at S R Nathan School of Human Development and chairs the COC-SUSS Certificate Course in High Performing Charities. In 2019, she authored the book titled *Building Enabled Communities in Singapore*. She currently studies and researches into social impact analysis, community building and engagement, and informal care networks. She teaches sustainability marketing, and non-profit management subjects like fundraising, volunteer management and maximising human capital for social impact. Her service to the community includes her position as an office bearer in HCA Hospice Limited, being a member of the SingHealth Community Partnership Council and a volunteer in reformative training.

Millie Yun Su is Head of Programme of Human Resource Management Programme in S R Nathan School of Human Development, SUSS. She received her PhD in Management from Rutgers Business School, United States.

Millie teaches strategic human resource management, business strategy, stakeholder management in non-profits, and qualitative research methods. Her research uses interviews and field observations to build theories grounded in the field, and she writes case studies for teaching purposes. Her research interests include issues in strategic management and human resource management in profit and non-profits organisations, volunteer management, and community building for caregivers.

Hock Lin Sng is an Associate Faculty at S R Nathan School of Human Development (NSHD). He teaches one of the course modules in the Graduate Diploma in Organisation & Leadership for Social Change offered by NSHD. Hock Lin is pursuing his PhD in Gerontology at SUSS. He obtained his Masters in Gerontology from SUSS, where he graduated top of cohort and was awarded the Alice Lim Memorial Fund Gold Award.

Additionally, Hock Lin is Chief of ActiveSG, Singapore's national movement for sports. Since taking over the role in 2020 he has led the transformation of the organisation, which has a staff strength of 700 personnel based in 26 Sports Centres, approximately 2.1 million members and 30,000 volunteers, to promote active living and community engagement through sports.

Before joining ActiveSG, Hock Lin was a Colonel in the Singapore Armed Forces. He was the Commander for Army Logistics Training Institute (ALTI). Under his leadership, ALTI collaborated with Institutes of Higher Learning to build an integrated educational ecosystem for servicemen.

For transforming ALTI with future-ready adult learning strategies, curriculum and training technology, Hock Lin was awarded the Public Sector Transformation Award in 2019.

Hock Lin volunteered with the Silver Caregivers and The Good Life Cooperatives. He was SUSS Gerontology Alumni Chairman (2018–2020), and is currently the Deputy Chairman of Singapore Polytechnic's Media, Art and Design School Academic Advisory Committee.

He graduated from Nanyang Technological University with a bachelor's degree in Mechanical Engineering. His academic qualifications further include Master degrees in Training and Development from Griffith University, and Transportation Management System from the National University of Singapore, Specialist Post-Graduate Diploma in Learning and Instruction from the National Institute of Education.

Acknowledgement

We stand on the shoulders of giants. This book builds on the exemplary work of scholars, leaders, and practitioners in non-profit management and leadership in Singapore and internationally. Many of them have gone out of their ways to help us along the journey to this book.

Our heartfelt appreciation to Professor Tsui Kai Chong, Associate Professor Lim Lee Ching, and Associate Professor Teng Su Ching at the Singapore University of Social Sciences (SUSS) for their guidance. Associate Prof David Ng and Associate Prof Ng Pak Tee from National Institute of Education for their sharing on Complexity, Instructional Leadership, and Organisational Learning; Prof Sarojni Choy and Prof Stephen Billet (Griffith University, on Workplace and Adult Learning); and Dr Reuben Ng (Lee Kuan Yew School of Policy, National University of Singapore, on data analytics and research). Dr Daniel H. Kim, Tay Kian Seng, and Andre Koh helped deepen our understanding of Systems Thinking, Leadership, and Organisation Development.

We are grateful for the trust and friendships forged with graduates from the SUSS's Graduate Certificate in Organisation & Leadership for Non-Profits and the COC-SUSS Certificate in High Performing Charities, including Beh Keng Hua, Charlotte Goh, Christina Cheng, David Lee, Eddie Neo, Foo Kok Wan, Lily Yeo, Michelle Nisha, and Tam Ching Yi. Their valuable insights, experiences, and reflections are the motivation behind this book.

Special thanks to Charlotte Goh, Christina Cheng, and Goh Tong Pak, who contributed examples in the book chapters. Ms Goh who is the CEO of Playeum, shared how her non-profit organisation pivoted at the height of the COVID-19 pandemic; Ms Cheng, Director of

Theory of Constraints for Education in Singapore, gave insights into prison rehabilitation; and Mr Goh, President of BreadTalk Group Special Project, shared his experiences and wisdom generously, such as his transformation journey as the former Principal of Xinmin Secondary School.

Writing a book demands significant detail orientation. We are grateful to Suhana Singh Madia and Valerie Kwan. They helped to peruse the appendices, figures, and drawings throughout the book manuscript.

We are grateful for many case examples which inspired us when writing this book. Our sincere thanks to many of you who have helped us one way or another, your passion and conviction for social good, drive us to do our part.

This book has also benefitted from the advice of Jiang Yulin at World Scientific Publishing Co. We bear responsibility for all remaining deficiencies. We aspire to work towards subsequent editions of this book and other publications that will contribute to advancing practice.

We are proud to be affiliated with the SUSS for its vision of contributing to social good through research in social sciences. Three of us got to know each other at SUSS. Our paths crossed in light of our shared ambition for a more robust social sector. This book represents the synergy of our pluralistic learning, lessons, and life experiences.

Finally, we are eternally grateful to our families for their support, patience, and encouragement throughout the writing of this book.

All glory to God!

Contents

Chapter 1
Setting the Stage

1.1 Introduction

The year was 2018 when she relocated to Singapore with her family. In this tropical island state, she found employment with one of the charity organisations founded by her home country. Let us call her Mdm B. Motivated to learn more about the charities and non-profit sector, Mdm B signed up for one of the executive courses I conducted. After class one evening, she stayed back, hoping that I could resolve her confusion about the diversity of actors and players in the non-profit sector here.

Try as she might to understand, she remained confused by our society's obsessive-compulsive use of acronyms from entity names to funding schemes. I did my best to explain, and our discussion concluded with her polite "thank you" before we parted ways. From the look in her eyes, I knew I had not fully addressed her doubts. This unresolved tension continues to haunt and drive me in my teaching and research up till today.

The inspiration for this book was conceived when the three of us began conducting research, teaching, and consulting for the non-profit sector in Singapore. Those incessant questions, curiosity, and "sparkle" in the eyes kept us going. We find meaning in designing and facilitating learning experiences to achieve what Aristotle termed "anagnorisis" — the discovery of something crucial that the protagonist of a novel plot was previously ignorant of, which led to a reversal of a complicated story (Kenny, 2013). Designing and facilitating these learning experiences that can help students discover solutions, synthesise abstract concepts, and apply them to challenges and issues in pursuit of their social mission fuel our labour.

1

The more we teach, the more in-depth we journey into research and the more extensively we consult. This learning, application, and reflection cycle reinforced our unanimous conclusion that there is not enough literature about management and leadership in non-profits in Singapore. Not enough has been written for non-profits in this part of the world.

There exists a copious amount of literature about the non-profit landscape in the United Kingdom, United States, India, Japan, Taiwan, Australia, etc. Yet, literature that is appropriate and suitable for our context pale in comparison. There are variations in context at the sector level, such as between non-profit and for-profit entities and across geographical regions. A nursing home in Taiwan may share a similar mission to providing a warm and loving living environment to the elderly with mobility issues as a nursing home here. Irrespective, the regulations and policies, social and cultural practices contrast vastly in both operating contexts. As a result, one requires different management and leadership skills to adapt, operate, and perform under each context.

1.2 A Common Language and Shared Meaning

This book aims to address part of the knowledge and literature gap we observed. Our goal is to serve some of this gap in writing about non-profit management and leadership for executives in the non-profit sector. Executives in for-profit organisations, especially those in corporate social responsibility functions, would find this book helpful to draw insights into non-profits in Singapore. This book also gives us a common language and shared meaning for the many words and jargon thrown around in the drive for transformation in the non-profit sector.

For the majority, the terminologies and concepts that you will read in this book are not new, but the environment and context differ. As an example, social service agencies commonly refer to their beneficiaries as clients. In the commercial setting, the client or customer is the reason for being, the purpose of existence. Hence, companies strive to retain their clients and keep them returning for more. For a non-profit organisation (NPO) like a social service agency that pro-vides financial assistance to the poor and marginalised, the needs of their clients are paramount. Unlike for-profit organisations, the end-in-mind is not to retain these clients perpetually on financial assistance. Instead, the goal is to empower these clients to be financially independent and minimise their dependence on the NPO.

As such, managing and leading an NPO is often more complex than a for-profit entity. A common management language can miti-gate the complexity and ensuing confusion. Within an organisation, a common management language adopted by employees establishes shared meanings across individuals and between hierarchical layers of the organisation. Management terms must be carefully defined and conveyed for communication with understanding. Action with under-standing gives purpose. Purposeful actions are necessary within an organisation or intra-organisation as well as between organisations, such as in a coalition.

Words like strategy, impact, governance, and best practice can carry different meanings for different persons and be interpreted dif-ferently. As a result, inferences made are at times erroneous and, worst still, action taken incoherent. Take the management terminology — "best practice". Some managers rationalise their recommendations for change by citing best practices. Without contextualising manage-rial recommendations to the organisation, citing a best practice as the reason for decision-making seems like a mindless copycat tactic.

Most of us who did not take business management at the under-graduate or postgraduate level, learned management and leadership through trial and error. We also learned by role modelling behaviours observed at work. More often than not, these behaviours that we observed are shaped by the organisation culture and the industry cli-mate. Thus, a common language and shared meaning are fundamen-tal to achieve alignment, shared meaning and purpose, organisation performance, learning, and growth. Imagine the time saved from misunderstandings, missteps, and missed opportunities when mes-sages can be communicated accurately down the command line. More significantly, the time saved can be spent to build trust among indi-viduals and between organisational hierarchy.

1.3 Strategic Dilemma

COVID-19 pandemic accelerated remote working and digitalisation. Consequently, operations are more complex, which means digitisation, digitalisation, and digital transformation are even more essential to be productive and proficient in achieving the organisation mission. Hitherto many organisations are resistant to the shift. One of the reasons cited is the perceived dichotomy between hi-tech and hi-touch. This dichotomy arose due to a misperception that technology and digitalisation displace human touch and thus depersonalise interactions. Eliciting such dilemmas is vital to help us uncover inertia to change and confront them to break the hold on static thinking.

Hi-tech and hi-touch are not separate and independent entities, Rather, technology and personalisation co-exist on a continuum. For example, Food from the Heart (FFTH) is a food charity that distributes food packs to the disadvantaged. In 2019, FFTH issues each beneficiary a physical card bearing the beneficiary's unique QR code. A volunteer of FFTH scans the QR code each time s/he delivers the food pack to the beneficiary. When a beneficiary visits FFTH's community shop to pick up food rations, the beneficiary scans the QR code on his/her card. With this simple technology, the food charity has insight into their beneficiaries' preferences, including collection patterns and consumption rates. With insights into the beneficiary's behaviour and preferences, FFTH can ensure that relevant food items are available for the beneficiary at the right time. With access to beneficiary's digital records, all FFTH staff can promptly meet the particular beneficiary's requirements.

The FFTH example shows that technology enables employees and volunteers to focus on meaningful interactions and even enhances personalisation. Reframing the tyranny of hi-tech or hi-touch into one in which hi-tech and hi-touch co-exist reduces the seemingly opposing forces of both ideas.

NPOs in Singapore are confronted with other strategic dilemmas. Example, mission and purpose or means, and preservation, government funding or philanthropic funds, employee-led or volunteer-led, change or stability, programme-driven or cause advocacy, data-driven or passion-focused, short-term or long-term goals. The list is countless.

In their book "Built to Last: Successful Habits of Visionary Companies", Collins and Porras (2005) explained that visionary companies embrace the "Genius of the And" concept. These companies determine a way to have both extremes or seemingly contradictory ideas simultaneously. They do so not through balancing between both ideas or blending the two in equal proportion. Instead, a visionary company sets a big hairy audacious goal and concurrently implements incremental and evolutionary progress.

We can embrace the "Genius of the And" and confront the "Tyranny of the Or" with effective managerial capabilities and leadership. This book introduces some of the relevant management frameworks and concepts that will boost the capacity of your managers and leaders.

1.4 Management Frameworks and Concepts

1.4.1 *Non-Profit Ecosystem*

To learn the management frameworks and concepts for non-profit management and leadership, we introduce the local non-profit ecosystem and the stakeholder groups in Chapter 2. The "5C Framework" typically applied in marketing to understand markets is used to frame the ecosystem and its constituent stakeholders.

Although we use the framework applied to understand business markets, organisations in the non-profit sector differ from for-profit and government-linked entities. A distinction that sets an NPO apart from businesses and governmental agencies is its organisation character, or more aptly, its heart and soul. NPOs serve the community's needs; charities and Institutions of a Public Character (IPCs) among them are founded for charitable causes. Essentially, prospective employees, volunteers, and donors are drawn to the heart and soul of the particular NPO. NPOs, including charities, must articulate and communicate their vision, mission, and purpose through their public outreach, deeds, programmes, and services to appeal to reinforce their legitimacy.

Why is this of significance? Human capital and financial capital are two crucial and invaluable resources for an NPO. Unlike for-profit organisations, most NPOs and charities lack the required financial capital to draw talent with high salaries and handsome benefits. So, organisational culture and mission become a crucial differentiator for NPOs and charities in recruitment and retention.

1 4.2 *Strategy for Growth and Development*

In Chapter 3, we will learn about strategy in the context of an NPO. Strategy formulation is crucial since a well-articulated strategy will chart the direction for every employee, including the organisation's volunteers. Strategy for a business articulates how the firm wins market share by winning over more customers through the firm's unique value proposition that customers are willing to pay (more) for. This is a limited view of strategy.

Simply put, strategy is about prioritisation, making choices, and trade-offs. Organisations across non-profit, profit, and public sectors have to make choices for their actions and the resource configuration. Strategy is not the same as activities or the operations of programmes and services that NPOs conduct for their clients. How does strategy formulation differ in an NPO *vis-a-vis* a profit organisation?

The crisis intervention hotline by the Samaritans of Singapore (SOS) (https://www.sos.org.sg/) is manned by volunteers who are unpaid labour. These volunteers are trained by the SOS, but they are not professional counsellors. Instead, they come from all walks of life, and they keep the hotline operating throughout the day and every day of the year, including public holidays. These volunteers maintain their anonymity, so callers do not know who they are.

This differs from another hotline that volunteers operate at Care Corner (https://www.carecorner.org.sg/). Volunteer counsellors operate the hotline for 12 hours daily (except public holiday) for individuals troubled by personal challenges, including issues related to family dynamics, grief, and loss, mental health challenges, pre-marital and marital concerns. Unlike the SOS, the names and qualifications of these volunteer counsellors are publicly available on Care Corner's website.

The mission of SOS is "to be an available lifeline to anyone in crisis", while the mission of Care Corner is "building hope and promoting well-being of individuals and families in community through social and healthcare services". These different strategic choices reflect the vision, mission, and purpose of the respective NPO. Additionally, the choices impact activities each organisation undertakes and the manpower, monetary, and non-monetary resources required and configured to conduct the activities.

1.4.3 *Stakeholder Management*

A social enterprise describes a company with a dual bottom-line, i.e., financial and social (or environment). Like charities, social enterprises direct or reinvest their operating surplus to social causes. Nevertheless, unlike charities, their dominant income streams are from programme fees and trading revenue. Hence, social enterprises in Singapore are not regulated like charities and IPCs. The majority of social enterprises here are registered as private limited companies.

The Singapore Centre for Social Enterprise (raiSE Ltd) defines social enterprise "as a business entity established with clear social goals and where there is clear management intent as well as resources allocated to fulfil its social objectives" with at least 20% of resources committed for reinvestment towards social impact (https://www.raise.sg/). In a landscape study of local social enterprises conducted between February to September 2020 and commissioned by raiSE jointly with the British Council,[1] there are an estimated 2,660 social enterprises here. Of the 146 sampled in the study, three-quarters of them operated with less than S$250,000 in annual revenue in the most recent financial year, about two-thirds (65%) run with one to five employees, and only 11% supported more than 1,000 beneficiaries over the last 12 months.

---

[1] *Source*: The State of Social Enterprise 2021 by raiSE Ltd (access: https://www.raise.sg/images/The-State-of-Social-Enterprise-2021_FINAL.pdf).

Regardless of the type of organisation entity, the size of an organisation can constrain its scale and scope, especially so in the drive for sustainable social outcomes. One single entity alone is unlikely to achieve positive and sustainable social outcomes and impact. Stakeholder management in non-profit settings is consequently an essential but often neglected topic.

We discuss stakeholder management in non-profit settings in Chapter 4. Like the story of David and Goliath, NPOs that operate with a small budget and employee size can punch above their weight and create mutually rewarding outcomes in the face of powerful and domineering resource-rich stakeholders. Drawing from extant literature on stakeholder management, the chapter determines four key steps of stakeholder management to leverage the power and strength of each stakeholder to establish cooperative relationships.

1.4.4 *Learning Organisation*

A comprehensive strategic plan and a vivid, coherent organisation vision are inadequate if you fail to secure and nurture the right talents for your organisation. Chapter 5 segues into a learning organisation with a focus on human capital development. A learning organisation is not just one that allocates a budget for employee training and development. Instead, a learning organisation institutionalises continuous team review and reflection to expand the organisational capability and capacity. Learning becomes inherent in the organisation culture. We recommend that non-profits cultivate and transform themselves into learning organisations to stay relevant to the desired social mission and keep pace with societal change and the complexity of social issues. The chapter presents several practical tried-and-tested tools for you to cultivate individual, team, and organisation learning.

1.4.5 *Drive for Social Performance*

Your NPO's desired social outcome also has implications for your strategy. Are your organisational capacity and resources capable of achieving the desired long-term outcome? Attribution is by way of causality. Unlike contribution, attributing the social change to your intervention is hard to establish. If you cannot attribute the desired social outcome to your NPO's intervention, you are better off adopting a focused strategy to ensure reliable output results.

On the other hand, you may choose to collaborate with other actors in the ecosystem to contribute (influence) to solving the social problem jointly. Different social change strategies will affect your organisation's performance measurement and report to funders and/ or donors. We discuss this further in Chapter 6.

To be effective in making social change, NPOs need to install a robust performance management system. Chapter 6 presents the logic model and social enterprise balanced scorecard as practical frameworks to holistically drive social performance. We discuss the concepts of the logic model, including the theory of change, input, output, outcome, and impact.

A performance management system comprises strategic objectives and measures that a coherent logic model can provide. However, the logic model does not encapsulate the contributions of stakeholder participants, which the social balanced scorecard can offer. NPOs can articulate a compelling narrative that relates their purpose to governance and accountability with these performance management frameworks. This chapter further explains the formulation of social impact, challenges, and issues in assessing social impact. The chapter concludes with suggestions for the implementation of social performance measures.

1.4.6 Systems Thinking for Organisation Transformation

The final chapter uses systems thinking to consolidate the management frameworks introduced in the earlier chapters. Systems thinking is helpful for us in problem-solving and in making sense of the interdependencies, interconnectedness, and interactions between organisations and across sectors. More significantly, we can use systems thinking to dig into problems and unearth those root causes that would lead to enduring solutions.

The operating context of NPOs in Singapore is unlike the environment and context of NPOs in other jurisdictions, including those in our neighbouring region. The stress and complexity that we function under are unlike those that operate in other countries such as Myanmar, Indonesia, or the international non-profits. A deep appreciation of the social cause we stand for and systems thinking enables us to differentiate detail from dynamic complexity. This ability to decipher the type of complexity using systems thinking can produce the most efficient solution that would lead to enduring improvements. The concluding chapter highlights key management concepts and applications in systems thinking for non-profits.

1.5 Conclusion

While we set our objective to serve some of the knowledge and literature gaps we have observed, we are acutely aware that one book will not address the gap in its entirety. Therefore, we share a proclivity for continued improvement on our research, training, consulting, and writing so that we can jointly contribute to a growing and thriving non-profit sector. Thus, this book will not be the last — rather a beginning for more to come.

Moreover, it is also our hope for this book to spur many of you to pen your lessons, reflections, and insights about management and leadership of the non-profit sector that will benefit the present and future generations dedicated to bringing about social change.

Last but not least, the best way to use this book is to apply the management frameworks that we introduce in each chapter to your context and task at hand. While doing so may not yield an immediate answer to your problems, you would gain a more in-depth understanding of the situation by applying the frameworks. We encourage you to share how you use the framework(s) with your peers, colleagues, and us. In sharing, you will inspire discussions of your mental model and reveal hidden assumptions, marking the first step to building a shared vision for your desired social change.

As a Chinese saying goes, "a journey of a thousand miles begins with a single step."

References

Collins, J. C., & Porras, J. I. (2005). *Built to Last: Successful Habits of Visionary Companies* (10th anniversary edn.). Random House.

Kenny, A. (2013). *Aristotle: Poetics.* Oxford: Oxford University Press.

Chapter 2
Non-Profit Ecosystem in Singapore

2.1 Introduction

Value creation is a central tenet in marketing. The goal of marketing in a for-profit organisation is to create value for the customer, collaborator, and of course, the company. Value creation does not have to be defined in monetary terms like economic value added, return on equity, net income, or market share. Value creation can be non-monetary such as in community engagement, customer satisfaction, and social innovation.

In the non-profit setting, where the organisation purpose is placed on benefitting others, value creation can be expressed in outcomes and social impact. Outcome is at the individual level when the non-profit organisation (NPO) fulfils the goal of individual beneficiaries. Impact refers to a sustained significant change measured by change at the community level, population or ecosystem level (Ebrahim & Rangan, 2014) such as improvements in human development indicators. We discuss outcomes and social impacts in-depth in Chapter 6 on driving social performance.

Beyond value creation in non-monetary terms, there are further general differences between organisations in the non-profit sector against those in the profit and public sectors. In this chapter, we identify the character of an NPO as a key distinction which marks the soul of the organisation. From the organisational perspective, we then move into the sector at-large to understand the non-profit ecosystem using the marketing framework known as the "Five Cs" (5-Cs) framework, typically applied to understand markets.

2.2 Distinguish Non-Profit from For-Profit and Public Sectors

Unlike the non-profit sector, commercial entities in the private sector focus on profit generation to sustain operations and undertake high-risk ventures to build wealth for themselves and their shareholders. Strategic decision-making prioritises monetary gains including projected profit margins and the return on investment extrapolated, to allocate resources.

Besides income from investments, commercial entities derive their primary sources of income mostly from customers by addressing or creating the market need with their value proposition and market differentiator. To create shareholder value, for profit organisations also grow through mergers and acquisitions in addition to organic growth.

Government and public agencies offer public goods like street lighting, national security, public transport infrastructure, to individuals and corporations. In exchange, they collect tax revenues from individuals and corporations to invest in the national economy.

For charity organisations, any income surpluses from operations are returned to fund the charitable cause(s) and operations. Likewise social enterprises return income surpluses to fund social ventures. On the other hand, surplus earnings in commercial entities are distributed as dividends for the benefit of shareholders including the board of directors.

Unlike the income source of organisations in for-profit and public sectors, the income of charity organisations, particularly those that work directly with their primary beneficiaries, are supplemented by individual and corporate donations, funding and grants from grant-makers and public agencies. For accountability to donors, funders, and interested public, the same management discipline of clearly defined objectives and explicit measures for effective performance must apply to charity organisations and NPOs.

More significantly, by drawing on public funds and donations for the attendant higher purpose of benefitting others, NPOs must be prudent and transparent in their resource allocation.

2.3 Character of a Non-Profit Organisation

The late Professor Khoo Oon Teik, a nephrologist at the Singapore General Hospital, founded the National Kidney Foundation (NKF) in 1969 to help renal patients who could not afford the cost of dialysis.[1] Since its recovery from the public fallout in 2005, NKF operates 37 dialysis centres islandwide today and cares for 4,716 patients and beneficiaries as of 30 June 2020.[2]

In 1986, Mr Wee Lin started Sunlove Abode for Intellectually Infirmed by converting an unused chicken farm to house psychiatric patients who had nowhere to go and whose families and friends were unable to accommodate them. Today, Sunlove operates two homes for the intellectually disabled and a range of community services.

Professor Cynthia Goh, Dr Anne Merrimen, and Dr Rosalie Shaw started Singapore's hospice and palliative care movement in the 1980s to help end-of-life patients live their final moments with dignity and without pain. They established Hospice Care Association in 1989, known today as HCA Hospice Limited, with Prof Cynthia Goh serving as the founding President.

Food from the Heart was established in 2003 by Henry and Christine Laimer, an Austrian couple then based in Singapore. Mrs Laimer was moved to collect and redistribute unsold bread from bakeries to those in need after reading a news report about the volume of unsold bread discarded each day.

Ray of Hope is a charity and fund-raising platform started by Mr Danny Yong in 2012 to help residents in Singapore who have fallen through the cracks.

The origins and beginning of almost every charity organisation can be traced to the passion and desire of one or a few, to serve the common good; it is this passion that fuelled the setting up of the organisation. This marks the soul or character of a charity or NPO.

---

[1] *Source*: National Library Board, Singapore (https://eresources.nlb.gov.sg/infopedia/articles/SIP_1558_2009-08-29.html).
[2] *Source*: NKF Annual Report 2019–2020 (https://nkfs.org/wp-content/uploads/2021/01/NKF-AR-2019-2020.pdf).

2.3.1 *What is an Organisational Character?*

Character is often associated with an individual, his/her personality attributes, values, and beliefs. The field of organisation culture emerged in the early 1970s by management scholars who researched into organisational character. An organisation is made up of individuals. The quality of judgement and decision-making by the organisation reflects the competence, commitment, and character of leaders in management functions and the board of directors. In other words, the competence, commitment, ethical decision-making, moral behaviour, and personality of the organisation's leaders shape the character of an organisation.

Psychologists Peterson and Seligman (2004) refer to the character of an individual as "… individual differences that are stable and general but also shaped by the individual settings and thus capable of change." Many scholars consider character to be a multidimensional construct (Wright & Quick, 2011) that encompasses individual qualities which motivate desires and pursuits of common social good.

At the organisational level, the definition of character is consistent with the raison d'être or the reason of existence of NPOs. The pursuit of the common social good and the desire to benefit others is the essence of charitable objectives.

Extrinsic motivations like compensation, tangible rewards, and monetary incentives are the levers often used by businesses to attract and retain employees. Unlike businesses, the NPO's character is what draws donors, volunteers, or prospective employees to it.

Given the pursuit to benefit others in the community, NPOs like charities should appeal to people's intrinsic motivation and altruistic values to attract and retain talents unlike the use of rewards and incentives by profit organisations. This is not to justify lower salaries for managers in charities. Rather executive compensation should be competitive and must be commensurate with the scope of work, attendant outcome, and desired social change.

The appeal to people's intrinsic motivation and altruistic values connects them emotionally to the particular NPO's social cause. NPOs depend on people, who are their key resources, to exemplify and live out their respective missions and purposes. Therein lies the character of the particular NPO.

The character of an organisation includes its branding, but it is more than the external facade. Character encompasses ethics, ethical decision-making, and moral behaviour. Ethics has many definitions and a commonly referred to definition of ethics is the decision between right and wrong. Decision-making between right and wrong is arguably more straightforward than one between one right and another right.

We prefer the definition of ethics as one that distinguishes between different degrees of right. As an example, let us consider the financial assistance for medical expenses here. For the prudent allocation of public funds, only Singaporeans and permanent residents have access to medical subsidies in restructured hospitals of Singapore. To enjoy the government subsidies, we will be subjected to means testing that evaluates our repayment ability. Yet, many hospice charities provide free home care services to end-of-life patients regardless of citizenship and socioeconomic class. This humanistic approach considers death and dying as a common denominator that binds all mankind and surpasses what is required for efficient resource allocation, to comply with regulations and the laws of the land.

Viewed in this light, the expectations of NPOs to deliver the desired social change for the common good are as stringent if not more complex than of for-profit organisations with their focus on the bottom-line.

This brings us to the individual and organisational capabilities and capacities required for organisational performance to achieve the particular NPO's stated vision, mission, and purpose. Hence, NPOs have the duty to nurture their employees' growth and development to fulfil the desired social change through learning and development as well as to nurture ethical judgement and decision-making.

Learning and development is not all about formal training. The majority of learning happens on-the-job for an employee. In addition to formal training, it is important for leaders and managers of NPOs to identify appropriate development opportunities for employees. An effective buddy system, coaching programme or feedback system can be as effective to help employees practise and develop proficiency in skills required for their job performance. Job-related learning in the form of special projects and stretched assignments are as effective to help employees acquire social capital internally and outside the NPO necessary to grow in the role. Chapter 5 discusses a learning organisation in detail.

We now turn to describe an ecosystem in order to understand the NPO landscape.

2.4 Understanding an Ecosystem

The year was 1958 when China launched the sparrow campaign to eradicate sparrows who feed on harvested grains alongside three major pests — flies, mice, and mosquitoes. People across all provinces in China started to slaughter sparrows en masse in their bid to increase grain yield; they shot down sparrows from the skies, scared them away by banging pots and pans, poisoned them with pesticides. What followed was not the desired outcome but severe locust outbreaks as sparrows are the natural predators of locusts.

Using an econometric model to determine the impact on grain output associated with the sparrow slaughter and grain loss, Chen and Wang (2021) found that each sparrow killed was associated with a reduction of 3.3 kg of grains. The sparrow slaughter created an ecological imbalance that resulted in an estimated seven million metric tons of grain lost that could have fed about 28 million people, about five times Singapore's population today.

Rather than achieving the desired increase in crop yield, this ecological imbalance along with a natural drought and other factors, contributed to the great famine in the whole of China between 1959 and 1961. The unintended consequence of the sparrow campaign on grain production yield escalated in 1960 and subsequently abated. The decrease only became statistically insignificant after 5 years.

What I have described is a natural ecosystem that is both complex and complicated. Mant (1999) used the metaphor of a frog to describe a complex system while that of a bicycle for a simple mechanical operation. A bicycle can be taken apart and re-assembled to function as before. In contrast, when any part of a frog is dismembered, the entire system is affected.

Put it in another way, a simple ecosystem is like a pendulum, the force is passed from one to the other, the relationships and interactions are predictable and visible. A complex ecosystem is made up of more than two different actors and entities. Each is independent yet interdependent; thus a symbiotic relationship. The action of one actor or entity has both direct and indirect effects on others in the entire system.

2.5 Non-Profit Ecosystem

The non-profit ecosystem is made up of entities across the non-profit, for-profit and public sectors in a symbiotic relationship. For-profit organisations are a constituent in the ecosystem because they have a vested interest in achieving environmental, social, and governance goals. Within the ecosystem, the relationships between entities within and across sectors can be by way of resource flow and/or information exchange. While each entity functions independently, the interdependence across sectors and between entities suggests that a change within a sector can affect other organisations across sectors.

When the Ministry of Health (MOH) revised the public healthcare subsidy framework and introduced patient means testing in 2002, many health and healthcare-related NPOs like social service agencies experienced a significant shortfall in income. Meanwhile, this created opportunities for private insurers to introduce and market innovative health insurance plans that enable policyholders to avoid any out-of-pocket medical and hospitalisation expenses.

Besides the interdependence across different organisations across sectors, the objectives that many NPOs aim to address and solve are complicated. Performance objectives that are anchored on individual and community outcomes are more complicated than output measures.

Both individual outcomes and community outcomes are often hard to control. Financial assistance for individuals who lost their jobs in an economic downturn can address the immediate physical needs like food and living necessities. Such assistance tackles the symptoms instead of the root causes. The coordination, cooperation, and collaboration of a network of organisations across sectors — commercial, public, and non-profit — will be required to help breadwinners who have lost their jobs return to the workforce, regain their dignity, and sustain productive employment. Moreover, one cannot be certain to attribute the outcome, such as the gainful employment of the individual, to the intervention of one single NPO. There are also social norms and attitudes about unemployment that impact one's recovery from job loss.

Some used the label "wicked problems" because social changes are hard or almost impossible to solve because of ambiguity, the involvement of too many stakeholders, and numerous interdependencies with symbiosis. This makes it all the more crucial for charities and NPOs to avoid the silo mentality and look to be part of an ecosystem involving multiple key actors.

2.5.1 *Size of the Non-Profit Ecosystem in Singapore*

Now, let us review some statistics to gain an overview of the non-profit landscape, such as the size of the non-profit sector, to make sense of the scale and the scope of coverage.

NPOs, including charities, Institution of a Public Character (IPC), social enterprises, non-government organisations, statutory boards, cooperatives, foundations, and trusts, form a substantial proportion of establishments in the sector for community and social services. The establishments or organisations in community and social services are classified under the services sector which also includes subsectors like finance and insurance, information and communication, etc. The services sector is a major contributor to Singapore's gross domestic product.

From data published by the Singapore Department of Statistics (Singstat),[3] there were 212,000 establishments in the services sector

---

[3] Singapore Department of Statistics (https://data.gov.sg/dataset/key-indicators-by-detailed-industry-in-all-services-industries-annual?view_id=5f6f6575-ac3b-4737-a312-b8e1f2c67dd8&resource_id=4d8fa425-7b39-4781-a765-64674d8a1693).

Exhibit 2.1: Total Establishments in Community and Social Services, Singapore

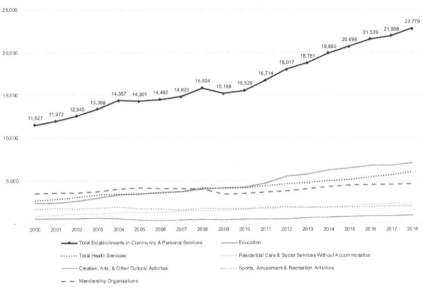

Source: Department of Statistics, Singapore.

in 2019. Within this sector, the number of establishments in the sector for recreation (including arts and cultural activities), community and social services following the Singapore Standard Industrial Classification (SSIC) (codes 85–88, 90–91, 93–94) was 22,779 in 2018,[4] a 4% increase from 21,908 in 2017.

The number of establishments in the sector (including education, health and social services, sports, arts and cultural activities) almost doubled to 21,908 in 2017 from 11,527 in 2000. Exhibit 2.1 is a visual representation of the trend in number of establishments and employment over the years. Although not all establishments in the sector are NPOs such as charities, IPC, foundations, cooperatives, and social enterprises, the overall trends, in the absence of detail breakdown figures, offer us an overview of the sector following Singstat classification.

---

[4] Singapore Department of Statistics (https://www.singstat.gov.sg/publications/ industry/sss-the-services-sector).

Along with the rise in the number of establishments, the jobs created and available in this sector are rising. The year-on-year change in employment for the community and personal services sector (including education, health, social services, art and culture) experienced a double-digit growth consistently for 27 years from 1991 to 2018, except for the year affected by the Severe Acute Respiratory Syndrome in 2003 when year-on-year employment change dipped to 7%.

Employment in the non-profit sector, including health and social services sub-sectors, is expected to rise as the COVID-19 pandemic turns into an endemic. There is urgency for organisations in the sector to uplift organisational management skills, capabilities, and capacities to respond to social-demographic shifts and technological advancements more efficiently and effectively.

2.5.2 *Charities and IPCs in Singapore*

Within Singapore's services sector, registered charities collectively represented 1% of the total number of establishments or 10% of the recreation, community, and personal services sub-sectors.

Charities and IPCs are tax exempt organisations registered with the Commissioner of Charities (COC) under the Charities Act (Cap. 37).[5] The charities in Singapore are commonly constituted as a society (under the Societies Act) or as a company limited by guarantee (under the Companies Act). Other organisational forms of charities include those created by specific statutes of parliament or through trust documents as charitable trusts for funds.

There were 2,281 registered charities according to the COC in 2019 which represented an annual growth rate of 1.25% between 2010 and 2019. Exhibit 2.2 illustrates the number of registered charities and the breakdown by sectors in the decade from 2010.

The COC segment registered charities in Singapore into seven broad sectors, namely (in alphabetical order): Arts and heritage, community, education, health, religious, social and welfare, sports, and others. Charities in the Religious (1,073, 47.0%) and social and

---

[5] *Source*: https://sso.agc.gov.sg/Act/CA1994.

Exhibit 2.2: Number of Registered Charities in Singapore Breakdown by Charity Sectors (from 2010 to 2019)

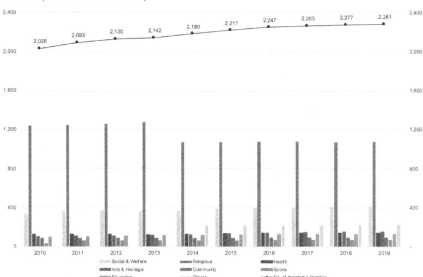

Source: Commissioner of Charities, Singapore.

welfare (405, 17.8%) sectors constitute two-thirds of all registered charities for year ending 31 December 2019. This is followed by organisations in sectors, as follows: arts and heritage (153, 6.7%), health (142, 6.2%), education (126, 5.5%), community (90, 3.9%), sports (70, 3.1%), and others (222, 9.7%).

Collectively these charities address different charitable purposes: Relieve poverty, advance education, advance religion, and other purposes to benefit the community including health promotion, arts, heritage, science, environment, sports, and animal welfare. Charitable here is defined as satisfying the needs of others in the community or the wider society.

2.6 Mapping the Non-Profit Ecosystem in Singapore

Given our 5.704 million resident population in 2019, there is one charity for 2,500 persons. A social purpose like health promotion is not one that can be addressed by a single charity or non-profit entity alone. The public sector plays an active role in enabling and empowering the NPOs to achieve their social purposes through a combination of funding, policies, and initiatives in capability building.

2.6.1 *Key Actors in the Landscape*

In the marketing domain, the "Five Cs" refer to five key factors that define the markets in which a business' offering compete in: Customers, company, collaborators, competitors, and context. We will use this "Five Cs" framework to identify the key actors and understand the non-profit ecosystem.

Social causes are part of the social mission, i.e., the NPO's reason for being. A social cause is the problem a particular NPO aims to solve in the community for the target beneficiaries. Social causes can include advocating for more scientific and systematic research into sustainable environment, life-limiting and life-threatening diseases, or can be direct intervention to address needs of marginalised groups including migrant workers and foreign brides.

Hence, the first "C" in "Five Cs" refers to customers. In a market economy, customers are the buyers whose needs and expectations the company aims to satisfy. The company, which is the second "C", manages the business offerings or solutions following its strategic objectives and available resources. The third "C" stands for collaborators. Collaborators refer to partners with whom the company work with to satisfy the customer's needs including suppliers, manufacturers, distributors, dealers, wholesalers, and retailers. "Competitors", who represent the fourth "C", are those who extend offerings or solutions to the same target customer segment. The fifth "C" is for context which refers to the external environment in which the company operates in, typically analysed using PESTEL — political, economic, social, technology, environmental, and legal domains. More about the PESTEL Framework is presented in Chapter 3. Exhibit 2.3 illustrates the 5-Cs framework for the non-profit ecosystem.

Exhibit 2.3: The 5-Cs Framework for Non-Profit Ecosystem

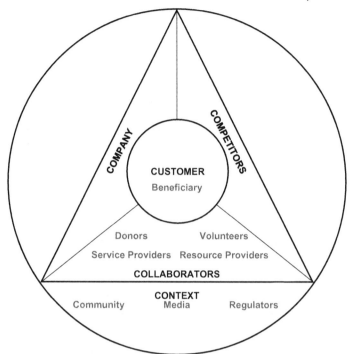

2.6.2 Applying the 5-Cs Framework in the Non-Profit Ecosystem

Now applying the Five Cs in the non-profit ecosystem, we have the following:

Customer. This refers to the primary beneficiaries whom a particular NPO aims to serve in relation to its social cause and mission. In the commercial setting, value is created when there is an exchange between the customer and the company for the business offering. There is an exchange when the customer willingly pays for the business offering at a price determined by the company. Moreover, the price charged commensurates with or exceeds the resources the company had expended to design, communicate, and deliver the offering.

In the non-profit context, although the NPO's beneficiaries are the target customers, the beneficiaries do not pay or only pay a significantly reduced fee for the services consumed.

For example, a charity or social enterprise that distributes meals to the immobile and isolated seniors dwelling in the community does not charge seniors for the meals. Such food charities mostly rely on individual and corporate donations to fund their operations.

There are dementia day-care centres that are registered charities in Singapore which do not impose the full fees for their programmes and services. For these organisations, the fees charged are usually net of government subsidies based on means testing results for Singaporeans and permanent residents. For these charities, their main source of funding are from government grants that is computed by a fixed rate per client. The fixed rate is insufficient to recover the cost of operations and these organisations are required to supplement their income with donations.

Donors including individual and corporate donors, contribute to the financial capital of charity organisations. The donation can be motivated by altruism or the emotional connection, in which case there is no value in exchange. On the other hand, there may be a reciprocal exchange like in a market tie-up when a business entity sponsors a charity to strengthen their brand value. Irrespective of donor motivation, donors are classified in the third factor, as collaborators.

Company is the particular charity or NPO that designs, implements, and manages the programmes and services to solve the social problems and address the needs of the primary beneficiaries.

Collaborator refers to a combination of service and resource providers, collectively referred to as "capacity builders" in the charity ecosystem (Cheng, 2008). Service providers may include professional firms such as accounting and audit firms, institutes of higher learning, IT advisory services, legal services, payroll administrators, strategy consultants, and training organisations. Besides intellectual capital, the resource providers channel resources including financial capital, human capital, and social capital. Donors, funders, grantmakers, and volunteers are resource providers, akin to shareholders and investors in the commercial context. Donors extend monetary resources although some impose requirements according to the donors' desires and interests; in practice, this is referred to as "restricted funds". Funders including government agencies may award contracts to NPOs to address specific community needs. Example, MOH awards service contracts to NPOs to operate the new baseline service at elder-care centres to better serve community-dwelling seniors nationwide.[6]

A grantmaker is a registered entity[7] that awards monies to other institutions or individuals that are aligned with its values and priorities to conduct charitable activities. Some examples of grantmakers in Singapore are Ho Bee Foundation, Lien Foundation, The Community Chest, Tote Board, and Yayasan Mendaki.

Volunteers offer their time, expertise, and network, contributing to human capital and some drawing into their social capital for the charity organisations they support. The types of volunteer functions can be broadly categorised into event-based, service-based, or skill-based. Event-based volunteers supplement the manpower needs of ad hoc events by the NPO. Service-based volunteers complement the work of practitioners and professionals in NPOs, e.g., befrienders, medical escorts. Skill-based volunteers lend their skills and expertise to the NPOs, e.g., hairstylist, web designer, sound engineer, management consulting, corporate governance. The board directors who serve in charity organisations are akin to skill-based volunteers who are not remunerated for the fiduciary duties they performed and many further contribute financially to support the charity.

These collaborators build the capacity and capabilities of NPOs helping to enhance their financial, human, and intellectual capital in order to more effectively fulfil their social missions and purposes. In collaboration with the NPOs, they expand the capacity of the organisation, which increases the scale of their objectives (i.e., number of

---

[6] *Source*: Ministry of Health (https://www.moh.gov.sg/news-highlights/details/implementation-of-new-baseline-service-at-eldercare-centres-for-all-seniors).

[7] *Source*: Inland Revenue Authority of Singapore (https://www.iras.gov.sg/irashome/Other-Taxes/Charities/Tax-Deduction-Scheme-for-Grantmakers/).

beneficiaries), and/or they enhance the organisational capabilities, which enlarges their scope. For example, the scope of services offered by Sunlove Home was subsequently enlarged from a residential home for psychiatric patients to day-care facilities for seniors diagnosed with mild to moderate dementia.

Competitors in the non-profit landscape refer to peer organisations that target the same needs and beneficiaries like the particular charity organisation. There are many NPOs who serve the needs of residents in rental flats. By definition, these NPOs compete against peer organisations for beneficiaries. The situation is exacerbated when their performance measures for funding are based on outputs or the number of beneficiaries served. An unintended consequence is a situation of over-served beneficiaries. In reality, many of these NPOs distribute themselves geographically to reduce duplication of efforts although more efforts for conversation and collaboration can be invested to bring about positive social change.

Besides the perceived threat of peer charity organisations, some charities compete with for-profit organisations. For example, privately owned nursing homes and elderly day-care centres are increasing their presence in the local landscape. There are home hospice services provided by private medical practitioners emerging who compete with free home hospice services by local charities who provide similar if not better services at a fee.

While these privately owned service providers target the affluent segment who can afford the full fees, they are in direct competition with the non-profit service providers for the mindshare of the population. The services offered can shape public's expectations and demands.

The threat from the privately owned operators is real. Many NPOs also lack adequate management capacities because of underinvestment in capabilities and competencies in legal and compliance, public relations, marketing, and strategy. The organisation budget and resources mostly go first towards programmes and services for beneficiaries.

Many charities are also under pressure to compete against their peers who are charities and IPCs for the donor pool that appears to be shrinking. Charities also compete among themselves for donors. According to the 2018 Individual Giving Survey conducted by the National Volunteer and Philanthropy Centre (NVPC),[8] donation rates in Singapore decreased from 97% in 2004 to 79% in 2018. The survey sampled 2,100 respondents who responded to the question: "have you donated in the past twelve months?" As donation rates fell, total donations have, however, trended upwards to S$2.11 billion in 2018 from S$960 million in 2008; the average donation value per organisation per donor rose from S$300 to S$611 in 2018.

Meanwhile the number of registered charities in Singapore rose by more than 14% from 1,994 to 2,277 in the same period.

Among and between organisations in the non-profit sector, a more effective approach to collective impact is collaboration, instead of competition for donors and beneficiaries. Moreover, the increasing value of average donation from the survey by NVPC suggested an opportunity to better engage with individual and corporate donors to increase the gift value and the frequency of giving.

The substitute for competitors is complementary organisations (Bloom & Dees, 2008). The missions, purposes, and primary beneficiaries of complementary organisations overlap. However, they can be complementary in advocating for a social cause or in addressing the holistic needs of the vulnerable segment better as a network of organisations.

"Sustenance for Families: Fresh Food Distribution"[9] is an initiative to provide fresh, quality, and nutritious meals to disadvantaged families by a network of organisations, namely, YWCA, Yong-En Care Centre, the Social Service Office (SSO), Pekik Community Services, and Majlis Ugama Islam Singapura (MUIS), supported by Aries Fresh Pte Ltd. The network of organisations includes entities across sectors, public, private, and non-profit, and they complement each other with different organisational capabilities to serve the community.

---

[8] *Source*: NVPC (https://cityofgood.sg/wp-content/uploads/2020/10/IGS-2018-Media-Briefing-16052019-FINAL-v3.pdf).

[9] *Source*: YWCA Singapore (https://ywca.org.sg/families/sustenance-families-fresh-food-distribution-volunteer/).

Context is the external environment which the particular charity organisation operates in. Within the context, there is the regulator who enforces the applicable laws and establishes the regulatory framework. The COC is the regulatory body for charities and IPCs in Singapore. The COC appoints sector administrators who are government bodies like ministries, statutory boards, and public agencies, to assist the COC to oversee different charities and IPCs. The six sector administrators are: Ministry of Education, Ministry of Health, Ministry of Culture, Community and Youth, National Council of Social Service, People's Association, and Singapore Sports Council. The COC and the sector administrators form one of the stakeholder groups in the context.

The media is another stakeholder group in the context. The media watches the non-profit sector and reports on trends and developments. These media reports are critical in shaping public perception and trust.

The community setting resides in the context. Members of the public who are in the community, form a stakeholder group in the context. While the public are by-standers and its members not directly engaged with the NPO, they give legitimacy to the NPO. Their recognition of a particular NPO's contribution to the wider community assures the relevance of the NPO's mission and purpose.

2.7 Demographic Shifts and Economic Transformation

With an understanding of the non-profit ecosystem using the 5-Cs framework, we turn to appreciate the significance of the ecosystem.

At the time of this writing, the Department of Statistics announced the census results of 150,000 households in Singapore.[10] The Census of Population, which is conducted every 10 years, highlights social and demographic shifts that will exert demands on the NPOs and impact the supply of talent resources.

---

[10] Department of Statistics, Singapore (https://www.singstat.gov.sg/publications/reference/cop2020/cop2020-sr1/census20_stat_release1).

In the sixth census since independence in 1965, the total population rose from 5.077 million in 2010 to 5.686 million in 2020. The rate of population growth was the slowest against the backdrop of an ageing society. Demands for healthcare services and formal care facilities are expected to rise, however there may not be adequate supply of professionals and skilled practitioners to cope with the demands. Today, many health and healthcare-related NPOs already contend with the lack of manpower including professionals like doctors, nurses, and allied health professionals for their operations. This is a systemic issue which threatens the future organisational capacity of our healthcare and related institutional facilities and community care agencies.

How might the constraints in manpower be unlocked? Besides formal care rendered by institutional facilities, what about the informal care network in the community such as the role of families and friends? Can volunteers be trained to be a part of the informal care network to augment and add to the capacity?

Consistent with trends in a rapidly greying population, the census also reported an increase in median age from 37.4 in 2010 to 41.5 years in 2020. The proportion of Singapore residents aged 65 years and above rose from 9% to 15.2% over the same period. The mean and median age of our workforce will continue to rise in tandem with the elderly dependency ratio.

Our culture expects the young who are or will be economically active to care for the elderly. Findings from the latest census further highlighted an increase in the proportion of singles across all age groups, particularly among those aged 25–34 years as well as fewer babies among married couples. These social-demographic trends have implications for our community. With small household sizes, families will likely be challenged by the care for the elderly at home and if social support is limited, these families would have little option but to depend on formal care networks like institutional facilities.

In China, the 4-2-1 family structure refers to the co-existence of three generations — paternal and maternal grandparents (four elderly), two parents, and one child (Jiang & Sanchez-Barricarte, 2011). One of the perspectives of this family structure is the prospective gain for the single child as he or she will stand to be the sole beneficiary of parents and both grandparents in time to come. On the other hand, such a structure will burden the only child being the only one working and the major source of help and care for the elderly in the household. Judging from the current social-demographic shifts, the potential burden on our younger generation can be as significant.

We operate in an ecosystem. Hence these socio-demographic shifts have implications on individuals, families, communities, as well as organisations across the public, private, and non-profit sectors.

As more employees become caregivers for the elderly at home, how might employers engage them productively while ensuring employee well-being? How might NPOs step up their capacity to prepare for the social-demographic shifts and mitigate the rise in caregiving demands? How might this impact the organisational capabilities of NPOs? There are implications on organisational capacities and capabilities.

2.8 COVID-19 and NPOs Operating Model

The COVID-19 pandemic has accelerated technology adoption, digitalisation, and digital transformation, especially online fundraising and crowdfunding for charitable social causes. Digital marketing including online fundraising will be the mainstay for charities in their fundraising appeals. A consequence of digital marketing is the massive amount of data that is generated on user behaviour, usage patterns, and social networks in the digital space.

What are the foreseeable impacts on donors, volunteers, and prospective employees when a particular NPO lags behind in digital marketing or digital transformation? What are the fundamental considerations of the NPO's data platform for governance and data security as a gargantuan amount of data is amassed from the web, social media, email management system, and customer relationship management? Are NPOs analysing these online data to inform strategy and decision-making to better communicate, engage, and advocate for their respective charitable cause(s)? How might such insights be a leverage for more effective fundraising or for accountability? The analysis and interpretation of large scale data that NPOs are amassing online will require knowledge, understanding, and skills in relevant tools and technology about web analytics, social analytics, user behaviour, etc.

While NPOs are not competing for the best and the brightest with rewards and incentives, today's advancement in technology gives pause for NPOs to consider if there exists the necessary skillset among their employees to leverage data for insights and foresights into user and donor motivation? How might NPOs make themselves appealing to those with relevant digital or big data skills? How might NPOs position themselves to be an attractive employer-of-choice for information and communication graduates? How might NPOs be an enchanting harbour for those who wish to put their skills to use as volunteers?

Tzu Chi Foundation was founded in Taiwan in 1966. As it expands its footprint to the rest of the world including Singapore, Tzu Chi retains its heritage and is predominantly Mandarin-speaking in Singapore. Over the years, Tzu Chi analysed the volunteer profile and saw that they are losing their appeal among younger volunteers. Their strategy shifted towards bilingualism and they actively adopted different social media tools as part of their tactical outreach to youths in the community. Their communication collaterals including handouts, posters, and billboards are written in Mandarin and English.

How might Tzu Chi's volunteer engagement strategy affect the volunteer pool and impact prospective volunteer impression and expectation of NPOs?

As the external context evolves, customers, collaborators, competitors, or complementary organisations are themselves responding to the changing context. Being a company (refer to the 5-Cs framework discussed earlier) that is connected and plugged into the ecosystem, an NPO must evolve its strategy and enhance its organisational capabilities and capacities to stay relevant and effective while retaining its social mission or its soul — the reason for being.

In closing, this chapter explained what an ecosystem is and described the relationship between different actors in the non-profit ecosystem using the 5-Cs framework. With this understanding, we can concisely map out the stakeholders and appreciate the interactions and consequence(s) of one's action on other actors and the ecosystem. In subsequent chapters, we shall explore the strategy for growth and development, stakeholder management, creating a learning organisation, and the drive for social performance before rounding up with systems thinking for organisational transformation.

References

Bloom, P. N., & Dees, G. (2008). Cultivate your ecosystem. *Stanford Social Innovation Review*, 6(1), 47–53.

Cheng, W. (2008). The charity ecosystem. *Social Space*, 4–13. https://ink.library.smu.edu.sg/lien_research/1.

Chen, H., & Wang, X. (2021), Sparrow slaughter and grain yield reduction during the Great Famine of China. http://dx.doi.org/10.2139/ssrn.3832057

Ebrahim, A., & Rangan, V. K. (2014). What impact? A framework for measuring the scale and scope of social performance. *California Management Review*, 56(3), 118–141. https://doi.org/10.1525/cmr.2914.56.3.118.

Jiang, Q., & Sanchez-Barricarte, J. J. (2011). The 4-2-1 family structure in China: A survival analysis based on life tables. *European Journal of Ageing*, 8(2), 119. https://doi.org/10.1007/s10433-011-0189-1.

Mant, A. (1999). *Intelligent Leadership* (2nd edn.). Allen & Unwin.

Peterson, C., & Seligman, M. E. (2004). *Character Strengths and Virtues: A Handbook and Classification* (Vol. 1). Oxford University Press.

Wright, T. A., & Quick, J. C. (2011). The role of character in ethical leadership research. *The Leadership Quarterly*, 22(5), 975–978. https://doi.org/10.1016/j.leaqua.2011.07.015.

Chapter 3
Developing a Strategy for a Non-Profit Organisation

3.1 Introduction

The origins of non-profit organisations (NPOs) usually lie in the hearts of the founders and the belief and conviction of helping those in need. Many NPOs in Singapore, such as AWWA and Food from the Heart, were first started off when a small group of professionals and their spouses wanted to help the needy. The act began from the heart, with wanting to help the under-privileged. However, as the organisation grows bigger with more manpower, offering more services and programmes, problems of managing staff, logistics, and resources become more complex. Founders' realise that operating the organisation solely from the heart may not serve them well, as professional knowledge and management skills are required, to manage different aspects of the organisation.

Developing a strategy should no longer be an exercise limited to for-profit organisations, but also be carried out in NPOs with discipline. Managing an NPO strategically does not mean the soul and heart are taken away from the organisation and its people, but rather honouring its mission and original intent by being a good steward of organisational resources, and being of service to the stakeholders, including employees and beneficiaries.

3.2 Why Strategy is Relevant for Non-Profits?

In for-profit organisations, their definition of strategy, its execution and outcomes, are rather straightforward, because the purpose of their existence is to win by generating profit to achieve above-average performance compared to their competitors. Winning also suggests competition and that the race is finite with an endpoint to the game. However, for NPOs, their existence is to accomplish their missions, which is long-term and socially complex. How to define winning in the context of an NPO? Also, are NPOs competing with their peers?

The NPO's existence is to achieve a social mission. Winning is about achieving a social mission and having a positive impact on society. An NPO is in the game of fulfilment; a game that delivers human services to fulfil the needs of certain social groups or to optimise human potential regardless of their ability or inability.

Sinek (2020) in *The Infinite Game* pointed out a remarkable distinction of how organisations distinguish themselves from playing a finite versus an infinite game. When organisations are playing the finite game, they want to win, perhaps in a quarter, a month, or short-term time frame; therefore, they develop products or adopt strategies to win within a certain time frame. For instance, they may cut costs, avoid investing in training, or focus solely on the existing markets.

On the other hand, organisations that are playing the infinite game are not thinking about winning, but rather thinking about how to create a completely new game and how to inspire people so that they'd continue to play the game. As he put it, "playing an infinite game is not just looking outside the box but beyond the box." Organisations and leaders with an infinite mindset are not thinking about a quarter or year, but a generation (Sinek, 2020, p. 14); they are not thinking about winning but fulfilling.

The same concept also applies to NPOs, and probably even more so because the definition of winning is more ambiguous in a non-profit setting than in a profit setting. When organisations position themselves in an infinite game, their existence is not about short-term victory, but a journey to fulfil a promise, a vision, to advance a social cause or mission. Therefore, a strategy for NPOs in an infinite game is a set of coordinated actions that leverage on resources to fulfil the social cause with compassion and sustainability. It is an ongoing journey where each step along the way is to advance the cause.

3.3 Definition of Strategy

Strategic management scholars have defined strategy as *"… an integrated and coherent set of policy and actions that leverage on the resources and capabilities of an organisation to gain competitive advantage"* (Hitt *et al.*, 2017). This definition of strategy serves as a foundation, but we will contextualise this definition in the non-profit management setting.

A strategy contains:

- An integrated and coherent set of policies and actions;
- Use of resources and capabilities;
- Accomplishment of a social mission.

3.3.1 *Strategy is an Integrated and Coherent Set of Policies and Actions*

One key element of a strategy is that it entails a set of coherent policies and actions that guide the day-to-day activities and decision-making. To achieve the strategy, the activities conducted need to be coherent and integrated to satisfy the needs and demands of the beneficiaries.

Let's take Samsui Kitchen as an example. Soup Restaurant Group Limited launched a corporate social responsibility (CSR) project "the Makan Project" to provide meals for long-term care facilities for the elderly.

Food served in long-term care facilities for the elderly was criticised for a lack of nutrition and variety, and many long-term care facilities ran their own kitchens with limited staff and outdated kitchen equipment and time constraints. Seniors with low or insufficient consumption of nutrition are associated with frailty, weight loss, and functional decline; and since long-term care facilities recognise the challenge, they have limited capabilities to resolve it on their own.

Samsui believed that its strategy for CSR needs to be integrated with the core of the company's strategy, rather than one-off projects or events. Given its long history in food production and in the F&B industry, leveraging on this set of resources and experiences became the rationale to contribute to social good; therefore, Samsui recognised the opportunity in serving meals to the elders in long-term care facilities. Nevertheless, with its size up to 300 employees, it had to be skilful and strategic in integrating activities and deploying resources to achieve its CSR mission. At the time when the CSR initiative was launched around 2013, the central kitchen was utilising the downtime period of its existing kitchen staff and transportation logistic to deliver 30,000 meals to seniors. As the CSR initiative gained popularity with promising results, its director, Ang Kian-Peng wanted to play the infinite game and planned for a second central kitchen to serve more elders and long-term care facilities.

3.3.2 *Leverage on Resources and Capabilities*

The second element of a strategy is that the organisation needs to leverage on its resources and capabilities to execute the strategy. Organisations possess both tangible and intangible resources, which fuel their strategy and actions (Barney, 1991; Wernerfelt, 1984). Tangible resources include physical buildings, land, equipment, technology, financial capital, and other artefacts. Intangible resources include organisational culture and processes, reputation, social capital, human capital, and intellectual capital (which can turn into tangible resources).

The following are definitions and examples of intangible resources critical to NPOs.

Financial capital: Financial capital includes the nature and character of the revenue streams and financial assets instrumental to operational performance (Brown *et al.*, 2016). It is critical to the operational performance, and requires managerial capability to utilise, govern, and regulate it. In the non-profit sector, financial capital can come from government grants as well as donations from private companies and individuals.

To carry out its CSR initiatives, Samsui not only drew on its financial capital but also donations from Standard Chartered Bank, which subsequently supported Samsui in various charity programmes.

Intellectual capital: Intellectual capital can be a set of intangible resources collectively generated and possessed by an organisation; it can be defined as the sum of everything that everybody knows in an organisation. It can also be organisational knowledge, such as intellectual property, as well as the process and infrastructure to develop and manage such knowledge (see Chapter 5 for more).

Samsui's critical intellectual capital resides in food manufacturing at scale, which it has accumulated for more than 20 years. Therefore, rather than building a new capability for its CSR initiative, it leveraged on what it knows best, making food on a large scale and training new cooks to do so.

Social capital: Social capital is essentially the social relationships that can be instrumental to organisational success; it can be external relationships such as the ones with donors, policymakers, third-party service providers, and volunteers, or it can be internal relationships, such as the ones among staff, board members, and leaders. NPOs are particularly sensitive to the social context and external relationships (Brown *et al.*, 2016).

For instance, Samsui was able to leverage its existing social capital with suppliers of logistics and food ingredients and negotiate lower prices, which is not commonly accessible to charitable organisations. Social capital can enable stronger bargaining power and access to certain forms of inputs so that the organisations can enjoy economies of scale.

Human capital: Human capital is characterised as the knowledge, skills, and ability of the workforce; it is the sum of individuals engaged in the work of the organisation. Human capital is an unlimited, valuable, and relational resource. For instance, skills such as leadership, communication, organisation, and problem-solving can be categorised as human capital.

For instance, Samsui's key human capital comprises its chefs and cooks who have been skilled in making herbal soups and home-based Chinese dishes. Samsui created a positive feedback loop where their chefs provide training to persons who are incarcerated or persons with disabilities who may eventually work for Samsui or find employment elsewhere after graduating from the training programme.

We will now turn to the most essential part of a strategy, which is a social mission. The social mission that an NPO pursues gives its strategy meaning and purpose; it motivates people to go the extra mile, and it inspires people to be creative and forward-looking. We will now dive into the definition of a social mission.

3.4 Defining a Social Mission

All NPOs need to have a social mission that defines the reasons for their existence. A social mission also includes a cause that inspires and drives an NPO to organise its activities and leverage its resources to deliver benefits to the targeted beneficiaries and have a positive impact on society. The cause will be bigger than the NPO or even the entire society, which may require social change, but it gives direction to a future state that will motivate people to contribute and help advance towards the future. Some examples of social causes could be climate change, poverty and homelessness, social isolation among the elderly, and teenage cyberbullying.

Once a cause is determined, the social mission outlines the objective and the action principles by which the NPO intends to take on and advance the social cause. For instance, Lions Befrienders' (LB) social cause is to relief social isolation among the live-alone seniors in Singapore. Therefore, its social mission is to "provide friendship and care for seniors to age in place with community participation."

Another example is Food from the Heart, established in 2003 by a Singapore-based Austrian couple, who was inspired to relieve hunger among the poor and low-income families through redistribution of unsold bakeries from restaurants and hotels. Their mission was to "alleviate hunger by providing reliable, consistent, and sustainable food support to the less-fortunate through food distribution programs." Since founding, they have been developing and delivering a wide variety of food distribution programmes to elders, welfare homes, persons with disabilities, and schools.

A social mission is not a superficial marketing statement but rather outlines actions that are relevant, operational, and achievable, to advance the social cause. An effective mission statement should have two key elements: (1) define the impact that the NPO is driving, and (2) elicit inspiration for the NPO's stakeholders.

The mission statement has to define who the NPO is serving (with some description about their primary beneficiaries), how they are being served (i.e., through NPO's delivery of products or services), and how the NPO can make a difference for them, which defines the NPO's outcome. For instance, consider this mission statement, "to provide services to the homeless in XX county." However, this statement does not specify what the NPO intends to change for the homeless, or what could be the desired state that the NPO aims to achieve through its services.

A revised mission statement could be, "to provide services to the homeless in XX that enhance their self-efficacy, or improve the possibilities for them to find a job." A mission statement should be translated into the organisation's strategy, and be incorporated as the foundation for the organisation's policies, planning, and activities.

In addition, an operational social mission would outline the scale and scope the NPO is expected to cover. Scale determines the boundary of the problem that the organisation intends to address, such as by the geography or targeted population. Scope reveals the range of activities the NPO engages in to address the need as identified in the mission.

For example, with a mission of relieving loneliness among socially isolated seniors, the scale of LB befriending programme targeted any live-alone seniors in Housing and Development Board rental flats and purchased flats, and the scope was determined by the functions and activities performed by volunteers who conduct the home visits and befriend the seniors. In December 2020, the Ministry of Health rolled out a new model of a eldercare centre to serve all seniors nationwide. As a result, LB had to pivot their strategy — LB reduced the scale of regional coverage of the befriender programme and enlarged the scope of its services that include exercising and recreational services for seniors at eldercare centres.

One can imagine that the scale and scope of a social mission may change over time as an organisation evolves and accumulates more resources. What NPOs should consider is, "if the infinite game is about fulfilling a social cause, are you solving the problem, or are you working to reduce the size of the problem?" Fulfilling social mission is a forward-looking and an ongoing journey; therefore, to play the long game, adjusting the scale and scope would be a key strategy along the way.

3.5 How to Develop a Strategy?

After discussing the key ingredients of strategy, we will now turn to discussing how to develop a strategy, which begins with analysing the external and internal environment. If an NPO is playing the infinite game, then the NPO leaders and managers would learn to see environmental factors not as stumbling blocks or constraints but rather work with the factors or even use them to create opportunities. NPO leaders with an infinite mindset would think about how to build a better ecosystem with character and integrity, and how to promote and advocate for the social cause.

3.5.1 *Evaluating the External Environment*

A common approach to examining the external environment would be using the PESTEL framework, which allows you to scan, monitor, and evaluate the macro-environment. Exhibit 3.1 explains the PESTEL framework. The framework segments external environment into six domains: political, economical, social, technological, environmental, and legal.

Exhibit 3.1: PESTEL Framework

P Political	**E** Economical	**S** Social	**T** Technological	**E** Environmental	**L** Legal
• Government policy • Tax policy • Political sentiment • Political landscape • Global influence	• Economic outlook • Economic growth • Employment rate/ Unemployment rate • Disposable income • Consumer confidence	• Demographic profile • Social environment/ sentiment • Age distribution • Lifestyle • Culture & religion	• Technology • Innovation • Intellectual property	• Environmental restriction • Neighbourhood zoning policy	• Rules & regulation • Court system

PESTEL framework can be useful when leaders or entrepreneurs are starting a new organisation; it can also be useful for leaders and managers to assess impacts of a new macro-environment on existing strategy and even identify gaps in the current strategy.

For instance, a social service agency caring for seniors may conduct PESTEL analysis to assess how its operating environment is continuously being impacted by COVID-19. Analysis of technological trend would reveal that the agency may need to help convert elderlies to adopting digital technology, or the agency may need to ramp up its volunteer management because more people are willing to volunteer due to the lack of travelling opportunities. Analysis of political and legal trends would reveal that government may have new mandates or provisions to care for socially isolated elderly, or has imposed rules in elderly care centres over vaccinated and unvaccinated seniors. Having a clear diagnosis of the external environment is the first starting point to identifying a direction for strategy.

3.5.2 *Entry Barriers*

NPO managers who are considering to expand the scale and scope of an NPO's missions also need to navigate the entry barriers into the non-profit market, or the so-called social sector market. The social sector market is a part of the economy that provides all of the social services and products in any community and directly benefits society (Robinson, 2006). The social sector market is social in nature, and is highly influenced by formal and informal social and institutional factors. In social sector markets, NPO entrepreneurs and leaders need to be aware of the entry barriers, such as the following social, institutional, and cultural barriers.

Social entry barriers: Social entry barriers consist of social networks of relationships that could prevent NPO leaders and entrepreneurs from accessing knowledge, social capital, and other forms of intangible resources.

Examples of social entry barriers:

- Lack of access to beneficiaries, which could prevent NPO leaders from understanding their demands and needs.

- Lack of access to manpower such as service providers, volunteers, and labour, which could prevent the NPO from delivering its programme and services.
- Lack of access to community-based organisations, which could provide support and infrastructure for the programmes and services delivered to beneficiaries.

Institutional barriers: Institutions set the norms and order within a market and this type of barriers could prevent NPO entrepreneurs and leaders from knowing the rules, norms and values, order and practice of a social sector.

Examples of institutional barriers·

- Lack of access to political infrastructure, which prevent NPO leaders from accessing knowledge and insights from policymakers, regulators, and grant providers.
- Lack of access to local business organisations, which prevent NPO from access to donations and volunteers.

Cultural barriers: Lastly, cultural barriers like norms, languages, beliefs, etiquettes, practices, and any of the unspoken expectations could also play a role in NPOs' securing stakeholders' goodwill and trust. Singapore being a multi-cultural and multi-ethnic society, NPOs have to be vigilant in considering the norms and unspoken practices among different ethnic groups when navigating the cultural boundaries.

3.5.3 *Evaluating the Internal Environment*

For NPOs that are playing the infinite game, the leaders and managers would be good stewards of resources and willing to make-do with whatever is at hand to accomplish the social mission. They will want to make their vision a reality, and their actions will be driven by the passion and commitment to the social mission.

For instance, Food from the Heart, like any small- or medium-sized charity with less than 25 staff, used only 1.5 headcount of IT staff to transform itself digitally in 3 years. A charity of 18 years, once an organisation with analogue systems, has digitised and digitalised many of its administrative infrastructures, such as its beneficiary management system, food distribution and warehouse systems, and volunteer management system, among others. Food from the Heart believed that digitisation does not take their heart out of the service, but adopted technology so that they could be more efficient in delivering more of their hearts to more people in need.

3.5.4 *Strengths, Weaknesses, Opportunities, and Threats*

One common method to assess internal environment is through Strengths, Weaknesses, Opportunities, and Threats (SWOT) analysis, which consists of two parts, identification of the SWOTs and then identification of the SWOT interactions. Questions to ask in the SWOT analysis are as follows:

1. Given our vision and mission, what are the five most important strengths of our organisation?
2. Given our vision and mission, what are the five most concerning weaknesses of our organisation?
3. Given our vision and mission, what are the five most important opportunities that our organisation can take advantage of in the future?
4. Given our vision and mission, what are the five most important threats our organisation needs to be mindful of in the future?

Another approach to using SWOT analysis is to assess the interactions among the SWOT. Exhibit 3.2 illustrates SWOT and analysis of its interactions. The interactions include:

• Weaknesses and threats
• Strengths and threats
• Weaknesses and opportunities
• Strengths and weaknesses

Exhibit 3.2: SWOT and Analysis of Its Interactions

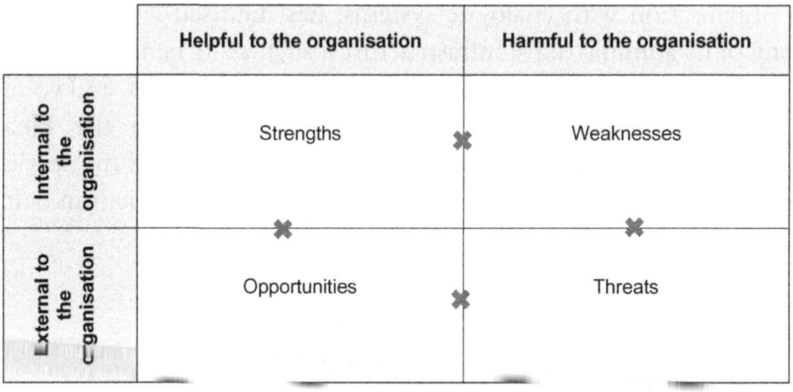

	Helpful to the organisation	Harmful to the organisation
Internal to the organisation	Strengths	Weaknesses
External to the organisation	Opportunities	Threats

- Opportunities and threats
- Strengths and opportunities

The interaction analysis may produce deeper insights that call for imminent actions or attention. For instance, when weaknesses interact with threats, such as manpower shortage and competition for volunteers is increasing, or weak fundraising capacity and government's cutting of funding, this would call for specific course of actions to mitigate the threat.

Similarly, interaction between strengths and opportunities would help NPOs look for leverage. A social service agency has a strong brand and more people want to volunteer, or it has an abundance of financial reserves and there is opportunity to expand its services. Interactions between strengths and opportunities could highlight the under-utilised resources, such as strong branding or better allocation of financial capital to bolster an NPO's strategy.

Interactions between weaknesses and opportunities could highlight any competency gap or resource shortage that prevents the NPO from pursuing an opportunity. Some examples of weakness–opportunity interactions could be: an NPO has limited capability in data analytics and digital marketing while donations and outreach have been moving towards online platforms and social media channels; or the board has not been active in fundraising solicitation while the social cause that the NPO advocates is raising public attention. In these cases, the NPO should consider ways to fill the gap, which may also lead to a new strategic direction.

When organisations consider how to win a short-term game, conducting external and internal analyses enables managers to derive a strategy that gives the company a competitive advantage to out-compete its competitors. But when organisations have a mindset of playing an infinite game, the analysis enables the organisation to know what it has at hand and how to work with the environmental factors to achieve its social cause. NPOs can also develop and accumulate an advantage but not to out-compete their competitors, but to bring in the right skills of volunteers and employees who resonate with the social causes and join the game with them.

3.6 Types of Strategies

Playing an infinite game does not mean that an organisation engages in all sorts of activities and missions without any focus. Successful strategy requires the NPO leader and managers to understand the trade-off and stay focused on its mission. An NPO can choose to broaden or narrow its scale and scope of social mission, depending on the external and internal environments (Ebrahim & Rangan, 2014).

Whether an NPO chooses to expand or narrow its scale and scope of the social mission, two key principles are important in determining which strategy to take: (1) leveraging on core competencies, and (2) building partnerships.

3.6.1 *Leveraging on Core Competencies*

All organisations should have a set of competencies that they can leverage on, which are called core competencies. Core competencies can be a combination of human capital with network relationships and technological or administrative infrastructure to allow organisations to excel. For instance, the core competency of HCA Hospice Limited is in delivering palliative and hospice care at home. With more than 30 years of experience, HCA Hospice Limited's multidisciplinary care teams comprise doctors, nurses, medical social workers, and trained volunteers who conduct up to 40,000 home visits per year. The patient's home is a part of the care system, where the care team of HCA Hospice Limited can function and adapt their professional skills in a home-based setting without any institutional fixtures. The care team also appreciates the uniqueness of each family's dynamics (i.e., socioeconomic status, faith, language, culture) and is able to communicate emotionally difficult topics with family members.

3.6.1.1 *Expanding scope*

When expanding the scope of its social mission, NPO leaders and managers need to ask themselves, "who am I," "why am I doing this," and "what do I believe in," to reflect on their beliefs, values, and personal convictions, and evaluate whether those are reflected and aligned with the NPO mission and strategy. The reason for founding of an NPO may be personal to the NPO's founders and leaders, which sits upon a belief and vision; therefore, staying true to the vision is what keeps an organisation in the infinite game.

The other two questions that NPO leaders have to ask themselves are, "what do we have" and "whom do we know," so that the organisation can take inventory of its resources, such as its knowledge, skills, capabilities, and social capital, and make use of what it has to stay in the infinite game.

For instance, HCA Hospice Limited's core competency differentiates itself from institutional-based palliative care where the patient may lose sense of control and dignity at a life-challenging stage. Instead of diversifying itself to compete with institutional-based (or inpatient) palliative hospice care, HCA Hospice Limited expanded its scope by honing in on its core competency in the community and deepening it by providing training to caregivers and volunteers so that more people could provide palliative care at home if needed. It also expanded its scope by partnering with counsellors, therapists, and social workers to provide patients and their caregivers home-based counselling services and art therapy.

3.6.1.2 *Expanding scale*

Knowing the reflective questions, such as "what the NPO is", "what it does", "what it has", "whom it knows", would keep the NPO on its course while reducing the risks of mission drift or misallocation of resources. Aravind Eye Hospital, founded in India in 1976, has a mission to "eliminate needless blindness" by providing large volume, high-quality, and affordable eye care to its patients in India (Ebrahim & Rangan, 2014). More than 50% of its patients received eye care either free or at a heavily subsidised rate while the hospital remains self-financially sustainable. In 2012 alone, Aravind performed over 340,000 surgeries and provided vision correction programmes to over three million people since its founding. How can it scale at this rate while being financially independent?

Aravind expanded its scale by establishing operational excellence where its surgeons could perform more than 2,000 surgeries per year compared to the Indian average of 400–500 surgeries a year. Its operational excellence also results from the assembly line approach to operation rooms where each room has a minimum of two operating tables with multiple sets of equipment and nursing teams. Aravind's core competency is in delivering high-quality, highly efficient surgical intervention, and it would be less effective if it moved upstream to participate in blindness prevention programmes because advocacy and marketing are not its core competencies. It was more effective and efficient at scaling up its mission by training more doctors and nurses from other countries and implementing the Aravind model around the world.

3.6.2 *Expanding Scale and Scope through Partnerships*

Another strategy to expand the scale and scope of the social mission is through building partnerships, which can be done without diluting or compromising the organisation's core competency. Building a successful partnership requires the NPO to continuously pursue its mission as if it is an "infinite game" and leverage on the strengths of its stakeholders effectively (more about the infinite game in Chapter 4).

Continuing with Aravind's story, the eye hospital believed that in order to increase the impact of its mission throughout India and globally, it had to scale to other developing markets with large impoverished populations. Therefore, it scaled by teaching others what it does best through training and research programmes with universities all over India as well as well-known medical schools, such as Harvard Medical School and Johns Hopkins University. It partnered with top universities in India and developed residency programmes for ophthalmology students. It offers training of "the Aravind model" to different professions around eye surgeries, including technicians, ophthalmologists, paramedics, and managers. And through various types of partnerships, it developed an ecosystem where all actors of eye surgical interventions can recognise "the Aravind model".

When building partnerships, leaders have to tirelessly share their visions with their partners. They also have to be open-minded and allow potential partners to co-create solutions. Recalling that Samsui's CSR initiative was a success in 2017, subsequently in 2018 Director Ang wanted to expand the scale and scope of the mission by reaching out to other groups of individuals in need and delivering up to 2,500 long-term care facility residents. In order to do so, Samsui partnered with Enabling Village where they co-created a CSR model, Samsui provided kitchen and cooking skills for persons with disabilities while Enabling Village provided the kitchen space and facilities, so that the trainees would cook meals for the needy.

3.7 Managerial Implications

Executing strategy has a few implications for managing NPOs. First, NPO leaders need to recognise that a lack of resources is not an excuse for the lack of discipline and stewardship. Managers have to recognise that they can have more resources than they think they have, and these resources may come in intangible forms such as cultural, social, and human capital. Instead of believing that they are resource dependent on the government, the NPO leaders can develop the ability to generate resources. Working with constraints may even trigger NPOs to become more creative and innovative. Second, defining a strategy is not a closed-door exercise among the NPO leaders and executives, but requires the NPO to engage with its stakeholders, including beneficiaries, volunteers, donors, and service providers outside of NPO, so that it can deliver an impactful programme and services that truly satisfy the needs of beneficiaries (more in Chapter 4).

Third, an NPO needs to have an efficient administrative and operation system to handle internal processes, which include a human resource management system that keeps its staff and volunteers engaged and coordinates their operations smoothly, as well as the capabilities to manage financial and intellectual capital effectively. Fourth, brand image and reputation are also a critical intangible resource that can provide strategic advantage. Brand image can attract donors and volunteers, and even attract credible and reputable board of directors to serve on the board. However, it takes years of effective programme delivery, engaging in partnerships and strategic marketing campaigns to sculpt a brand image, which requires a variety of social, human, and intellectual capital to cultivate.

Last but not least, NPO leaders and staff need to have the human capital to lead and to execute; moreover, they have to believe in the social mission. Leaders have to step up to lead and guide the organisation, communicate effectively with various internal and external stakeholders, including board members, policymakers, and funders. Staff must have the human capital to execute and solve problems; more importantly, they must have knowledge as well as the people management skills to deliver programmes and services with integrity.

The bottom line is that people and social capital are the most important resources in an NPO, and it is the people with managerial capacity who can deploy, organise, and configure the resources in a creative and effective way to achieve a long-term strategic advantage.

3.8 Challenges in Executing a Strategy

In this last section, I will dedicate some discussion on the challenges with developing and executing strategy. This chapter provides concepts and processes to think about organisational strategy more strategically. Nevertheless, a strategy is not always perfect and it could create dilemmas and challenges for managers. For one, all strategies have trade-offs, because an organisation with scarce resources cannot serve everyone and accomplish everything, so its leaders will have to face hard choices and decide what to do and what not to do. The consequence of not facing trade-offs is mission drift, where the NPO diverges from its initial mission.

Second, NPO leaders may face public good dilemma where they may decide not to cooperate or contribute to a joint solution that benefits the public good because of conflicts of interest. Such a situation calls for thinking and defining clearly about the outcome and impact the NPO intends to have. Without mapping out the outcome and impact, an NPO would only be dealing with symptoms instead of root causes (see Chapter 6 for further discussion). For instance, Samaritans of Singapore, a non-profit providing emotional support and interventions to individuals who are thinking about or are affected by suicide, is an example of an organisation that faces such public good dilemma. On the one hand, it has merits and benefits in helping individuals under emotional crisis and preventing them from taking their lives. It also means that Samaritan of Singapore's success would depend on the number of suicidal cases it deters; the more cases it prevents, the more successful it is. However, such an approach addresses the symptoms but not the root causes, which would require a very different strategy, such as advocacy, addressing specific common causes of suicide, or rolling out counselling programmes. However, addressing the root causes may be less appealing than providing services or training, because the outcome for the latter is more tangible, while addressing the root causes could require social change, change of mindsets, or changing of policies and institutions. As a result, an NPOs strategy could face a double-edged sword by driving its operational success without addressing the root cause of a social problem.

3.9 Conclusion

In conclusion, this chapter discusses the importance and the key elements of developing a strategy in a non-profit setting. An NPO is in the game of fulfilling human potential with human services. Understanding external and internal environments of the organisation is the first step to developing a strategy. Having a strategy that leverages on its resources and competencies also allows an NPO to develop an edge that attracts more talent and more resources to accomplish the social mission together. An NPO's existence is ultimately to achieve a social mission, and having a strategy to achieve its social mission does not take the heart out of the NPO, but rather extends the heart further to serve more people and create more positive impact on society.

References

Barney, J. (1991). Firm resources and sustained competitive advantage. *Journal of Management, 17*(1), 99–120.

Brown, W. A., Andersson, F. O., & Jo, S. (2016). Dimensions of capacity in nonprofit human service organisations. *VOLUNTAS: International Journal of Voluntary and Nonprofit Organisations, 27*(6), 2889–2912.

Ebrahim, A., & Rangan, V. K. (2014). What impact? A framework for measuring the scale and scope of social performance. *California Management Review, 56*(3), 118–141.

Hitt, M. A., Ireland, R. D., & Hoskisson, R. E. (2017). *Strategic Management: Concepts and Cases: Competitiveness and Globalization.* Cengage Learning.

Robinson, J. (2006). Navigating social and institutional barriers to markets: How social entrepreneurs identify and evaluate opportunities. In *Social Entrepreneurship* (pp. 95–120). Springer.

Sinek, S. (2020). *The Infinite Game.* Penguin Random House, UK.

Wernerfelt, B. (1984). A resource-based view of the firm. *Strategic Management Journal, 5*(2), 171–180.

Chapter 4
Managing Stakeholders in Non-Profit Settings

4.1 Introduction

In the previous chapter, we discussed that the purpose of a strategy is to achieve a social mission with the resources at hand and coherent actions. A non-profit organisation's (NPO) strategy is to stay in the "infinite game" and bring more people to contribute to the game. An NPO cannot accomplish the social mission alone, but must rely on partnerships in the ecosystem to fulfil its social mission. Therefore, in this chapter, stakeholder management in the non-profit management setting, is a process of involving others to advance the social mission together.

Stakeholder management has been a topic under-addressed in the non-profit management context, only limited in the executive management level, and theoretical concepts and tools are largely drawn from managing stakeholders in the profit sector. NPO managers face different stakeholders, each of whom bring forth different and sometimes conflicting objectives, yet managers have limited concepts or frameworks to approach stakeholders. This chapter aims to lay down the foundation in stakeholder management and provides key concepts for practitioners to analyse stakeholders and engage them strategically.

4.2 Definition and Purpose of Stakeholder Management

A classic definition of a stakeholder of an organisation is, "any group or individual who can affect or is affected by the achievement of the organisation's objective" (Freeman, 2010, p. 46). They are any persons, groups, neighbourhoods, organisations, institutions, or even the natural environments that have a stake in the organisation's performance, activities, and operation. For example, a social service agency (SSA) would have a wide variety of stakeholders, including beneficiaries, staff (both frontline and backend), volunteers, government policymakers, community leaders, neighbours and neighbouring environments, vendors, intermediary service providers (e.g., healthcare providers, ration providers, counsellors or therapists), corporate and individual donors.

In Asian context, managers, especially the ones in the non-profit sector, would find it odd or even calculative, to manage stakeholders "strategically", because relationship building in Asian cultures is known to be based on *guan-xi* (Chinese term for "relationships") and trust, rather than on interests and expectation. As a result, managers believe that relationship management only relies on face time, and would subsequently overlook the process of conducting stakeholder analysis and developing communication plans.

Being strategy at stakeholder management requires multiple parties developing mutual understanding for the social mission and bringing others to contribute to the mission. Successful stakeholder management starts with understanding the beneficiaries, the end user of your service. It requires NPO managers to have deep understanding of their needs, demands, and pain points.

Stakeholder management involves identifying the relevant stakeholders in order to develop coherent action to achieve the social mission collectively. A robust stakeholder management will enable managers to know their stakeholders, what is at stake for them, and be able to develop a win–win situation. The intention is to give each other an opportunity to establish a common understanding and build a long-term relationship.

Successful stakeholder management also requires managers to inspire others to participate; it involves others' understanding of the mission and the willingness to contribute.

Communication is the key to successful stakeholder management, where managers create opportunities to express their objectives, understand their stakeholders, work to find a common ground, and inspire them to contribute or participate in their objective. The rest of the chapter will outline the key steps to manage stakeholders effectively.

4.3   What is at Stake for the NPO?

Let's imagine what could be the consequences if an NPO does not manage the stakeholders well. One of the immediate consequences would be that the needs of beneficiaries are not met, are under- or over-served, which cause more social problems. Say an SSA has been ineffectively resolving disagreements between volunteers and its full-time staff. A poor management of volunteers as one of the SSA's key stakeholders would result in low volunteer retention or high volunteer turnover. Consequently, the SSA would have to spend more resources to recruit and re-train volunteers; the SSA would also lose tacit and institutional knowledge.

Another aftermath of unsuccessful stakeholder management would be reduction or withdrawals of corporate donors or mission drift. As more corporations are engaging with NPOs to fulfil their corporate social responsibility (CSR), they also want to see concrete outcomes from their partnerships. For example, they may request performance data to monitor the impact of their investment dollars on the social cause, or they may make specific requests in the philanthropic events to improve their employee engagement or elevate their branding through their partnership. If NPOs do not manage partnerships effectively, corporate donations may be withdrawn or reduced. Alternatively, NPO managers would comply or acquiesce to the demands of the corporate sponsors and expose themselves to potential mission drift.

There are two reasons why stakeholder management is especially important for NPOs. First, NPO managers have limited resources in terms of financial capital and manpower, yet they face a wide range of stakeholders, some may introduce conflicting or complicated interests. Without a stakeholder management strategy, the response strategy to stakeholders would become ad hoc or reactive, and as time goes on, operational responses could become incoherent or strategic direction may drift away from the organisation's core mission.

Second, NPO managers on a day-to-day basis face the continuous demands from external stakeholders such as beneficiaries or parties associated with beneficiaries (such as families, school institutions), volunteers, government, corporate partners, whom NPOs are dependent on for their survival. NPO managers would see themselves at the lower end of bargaining power. As a consequence, it becomes harder for managers to leverage or strike effective relationships.

4.4 Stakeholder Management: Four Key Questions

In the following section, we will outline four key questions that help managers prepare for stakeholder management. Exhibit 4.1 shows the four key questions central to stakeholder management.

To learn more about an NPO's stakeholders, managers need to answer and assess the following: (1) who are the stakeholders,

Exhibit 4.1: Stakeholder Management: Four Key Questions

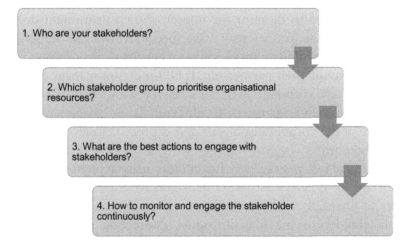

1. Who are your stakeholders?

2. Which stakeholder group to prioritise organisational resources?

3. What are the best actions to engage with stakeholders?

4. How to monitor and engage the stakeholder continuously?

(2) which stakeholder group to prioritise for organisational resources, (3) what are the best actions to engage with stakeholders, (4) how to monitor and engage the stakeholders continuously?

4.4.1 *Identifying Stakeholders: Who are Your Stakeholders?*

In order to effectively manage stakeholders, the first and foremost task is to identify who they are. There are several ways to identify and categorise stakeholders, in terms of their impact to the organisation, such as primary and direct, secondary and indirect impact and also according to the value chain. How you define the range of stakeholders to attend to has to do with how much resources and capacity the organisation has. With limited resources, an organisation may identify a more narrow or manageable group of appropriate stakeholders to manage (Mitchell *et al.*, 1997).

4.4.1.1 *Identifying primary and secondary stakeholders*

One common way of identifying stakeholders would be thinking of them as primary and secondary. Exhibit 4.2 illustrates primary and secondary stakeholders in concentric circles.

Primary stakeholders are ones who have a direct stake in the organisation and its success. They may have direct impact on the day-to-day operation of the NPO, or their continuous participation in the NPO's activity may be crucial to its survival; hence, they are highly influential. For instance, beneficiaries, staff, volunteers, and social and medical service providers have direct impact on an NPO's operation and service delivery to beneficiaries.

Secondary stakeholders are ones who may impact the NPO's reputation, responsibilities, and its public standing, without continuous participation in the NPO's operation. Secondary stakeholders may not have direct impact on an NPO's day-to-day operation, but they can also be quite influential with regulatory or financial power. For instance, an NPO's top executives and board of directors,

Exhibit 4.2: Primary and Secondary Stakeholders

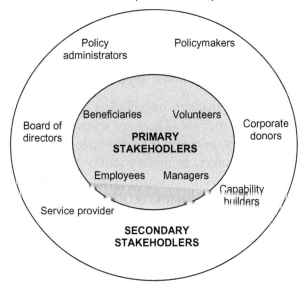

policymakers and regulators, grant examiners and administrators, and corporate funders and other related entities.

4.4.1.2 *Identifying stakeholders with value chain*

Another useful way of identifying stakeholders would be mapping them according to the organisation's value chain, which captures a set of activities which an NPO performs to deliver its services. Exhibit 4.3 shows different actors in the value chain of social service delivery.

A value chain of social service delivery can be broken into upstream and downstream, where upstream stakeholders are the ones making policy and strategic decisions, sourcing funds and donation, designing programmes, sourcing and selecting service providers, and corporate and individual donors. They may be internal or external to the NPO. For instance, policy decision-makers, corporate and individual donors are considered as upstream and external stakeholders, as they set the policy guidelines, evaluation framework, and the financial resources to allow the NPO to operate.

Exhibit 4.3: Value Chain of Social Service Delivery

Policymakers

NPO's, social service
agencies, charities

Donors
(corporate, individuals)

Staff, service providers,
community workers

Beneficiaries

Downstream stakeholders are the ones who have direct interactions with the beneficiaries, such as staff, service providers, and volunteers, and they may be internal or external to the NPO as well. For instance, contracted service providers and volunteers are considered as external downstream stakeholders.

4.4.1.3 *Identifying stakeholders by sectors*

Alternatively, identifying stakeholders by sector is also useful, such as people, public, and private, where each of them may have their own professional and institutional norms, mental schemes, interests, and expectations (DiMaggio & Powell, 1983). The differences across sectors could create fault lines in communication and expectations, and thus become a hurdle in collaboration.

For instance, private organisations have responsibilities towards their shareholders, customers, and employees, and they are more likely to prioritise profit and earnings; they also have higher expectations in terms of efficiency and productivity as they have more managerial and financial resources. Stakeholders from the public sector have responsibilities towards the citizens and the general public; they set the institutional guidelines to reflect on the national and public interests and hold the NPO's accountable to their missions and objectives. Recognising which sector the stakeholders come from would allow NPO practitioners to set the appropriate expectation, understand what their priorities are, as well as use a common language to interact and communicate with the stakeholders.

Once the stakeholders are identified, consider their claims, which can be a stake, an interest, or it can be a demand or expectation for something. When understanding the stakeholders, consider the following questions:

- What are the stakeholders' claim with respect to the social cause?
- What are the stakeholders' underlying demands and priorities?
- What are the stakes that the stakeholders are facing when delivering services to advance the social cause?
- What are the common grounds between their stake and the non-profit organisation's stake?
- What can the non-profit organisation do to help them with their stake?

Referring to Samsui kitchen discussed in Chapter 3, while Samsui provides meals for the elderly residents in the long-term care facilities, who are their primary beneficiaries, Samsui also needs to understand what is at stake for the long-term care facilities. The long-term care facilities faced difficulties in preparing delicious and nutritious meals for the elderly; they are low on manpower and budget for food preparation. Samsui had to understand the operation of the care facilities, their stake and challenges pertaining to meal preparation, so that its meal delivery could be well-integrated with the facilities' programme.

Therefore, considering what is at stake for the stakeholder could give clues about what prevents the stakeholders from engaging or partnering with the NPO. The answer to this question will also shed new light on the mindset of approaching stakeholders differently.

4.4.2   *Which Stakeholder Group to Prioritise for Organisational Resources?*

After identifying a wide array of stakeholders, the next question is to sort out which stakeholder groups deserve managerial attention at different points in time. Managers have to prioritise their attention because they have limited resources to respond to all stakeholders. Mitchell *et al.* (1997) developed a salience model that characterises stakeholders according to their attributes such as power, legitimacy, and urgency, to determine their salience. The more salient the stakeholder, which means that the stakeholder possesses two or three of the attributes, hence, the more priority the managers will give to attend to the stakeholder's demand.

The three attributes to characterise stakeholders are power, legitimacy, and urgency. Exhibit 4.4 tabulates the definition of each stakeholder attribute.

Power refers to the ability or capacity of the stakeholders to produce effects or to exert influence over decisions or agenda (Mitchell *et al.*, 1997). Power can come from financial resources, human capital, or social capital, which provide utility and give stakeholders the means to influence. Power can also come from legal or regulatory status. For example, corporate donors are powerful to NPOs because they possess financial resources that may support NPOs' operations or

Exhibit 4.4: Definition of Three Stakeholder Attributes

Attributes	Definition	Examples
Power	Ability or capacity to produce effects or to exert influence over decisions or agenda.	• Financial power • Utility power • Normative power (i.e., narrative, sentiments, public opinions)
Legitimacy	Perception or assumption that the claim is socially accepted or under a system of social values, norms, or belief.	• Filial piety • Caring for the elderly • Protecting the environment • Caring for persons with mental health issues • Non-discriminatory hiring
Urgency	The degree to which stakeholder's claim calls for immediate attention or response.	• Relief in social isolation among seniors during COVID-19 Circuit Breaker • People having intention to commit suicide

influence their agenda, even though they may not directly impact the organisations' day-to-day operations. Employees and volunteers also have power (utility, knowledge, skills) as important stakeholders groups that NPOs cannot ignore. While employees are formal staff where NPOs have responsibilities of their job and performance, volunteers provide utility power to deliver services for NPOs. Both have influence over the outcome and impact that NPOs want to deliver.

Legitimacy refers to the perception or assumption that the stakeholder's claims or demands are socially accepted or have fallen under a system of social values, norms, or beliefs (Mitchell *et al.*, 1997). For instance, beneficiaries who are the target of an NPO's social mission and service, employees, board of directors, service providers, are legitimate stakeholders who are bound by contracts or services. NPOs also have legitimacy in their social missions as they advocate for the rights and welfare of beneficiaries and raise awareness of certain issues.

Last but not least, urgency refers to the degree to which a stakeholder's claim calls for immediate attention or response (Mitchell *et al.*, 1997). It means that the claims or demand of the stakeholders is time sensitive and critical to the stakeholders. Oftentimes, NPOs are responding to stakeholders according to this attribute, particularly their beneficiaries who are in a place of urgent need. When NPOs are forced to respond to urgent needs of beneficiaries, the situation would either motivate them to be innovative or disrupt their existing operations.

While this is a model that is mostly applied in business setting, the three attributes, power, legitimacy, and urgency, have their merits in helping analyse the stakeholders in order to develop engagement strategies with them. Beneficiaries' claims and demands are salient in their urgency and legitimacy, while corporations and policymakers are salient in their power and legitimacy; therefore, it is important for the NPO manager to gauge the level of resources and manpower to address their needs.

When considering who and how to respond to the stakeholders, ask yourself the following questions:

- How can I characterise my stakeholders according to these attributes, power, legitimacy, and urgency?

- How do my stakeholders view me in terms of the three attributes, power, legitimacy, and urgency?
- How have I been responding to their claims and demands?
- What can I improve in terms of responding to their claims and demands?

4.4.3 *What Actions Should the NPO Take to Best Address Stakeholders?*

As mentioned in the beginning of the chapter, an NPO needs stakeholders with different expertise and from different domains to work together to advance the social cause, and stakeholder management is to manage their involvement so that the collaboration is fulfilling and effective. As such, engagement strategy with different stakeholders can be developed based on stakeholders' power to influence the NPO's operation and their direct or indirect impact on the beneficiary. Exhibit 4.5 shows different engagement strategies using the power–impact grid.

Power to influence is determined by the stakeholder's ability or capacity to exert influence over decisions or agenda, and the impact on beneficiaries is determined by their position on the value chain.

Exhibit 4.5: Power–Impact Grid

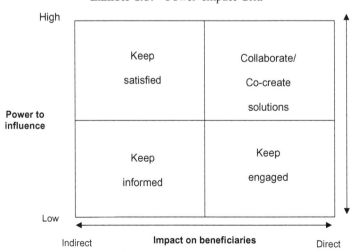

4.4.3.1 *High power to influence X indirect impact on beneficiaries*

Policymakers and regulators could be considered as stakeholders who have high power to influence NPOs' operations as they determine guidelines and regulations, but they have indirect impact on beneficiaries because they are in the upstream of the value chain. NPOs would want to keep them satisfied by fulfilling the policy requirements and demonstrating outputs and outcomes that they are achieving. Policymakers could provide key performance indicators that NPOs need to fulfil and it is important for NPOs to maintain their legitimacy and integrity. However, there are times when NPOs need to work with government agencies on defining a set of relevant outcome measures that will direct the effort to the desirable impact (more about this in Chapter 6).

4.4.3.2 *High power to influence X direct impact on beneficiaries*

For stakeholders who have high power to influence an NPO's operation and direct impact on the beneficiaries, the NPO should collaborate with them or even work closely with them to co-create solutions for beneficiaries. They could be staff, service providers, and even loyal volunteers who have direct knowledge of the beneficiaries. The NPO may mobilise their support and involvement, or even allow them to provide strategic inputs to advance the social cause. For instance, Tzu Chi Foundation is a charity organisation that effectively leverages its volunteers, who participate in a wide range of activities from front-end efforts in home visits and emergency responses to back-end efforts in publication and marketing.

4.4.3.3 *Low power to influence X direct impact on beneficiaries*

For stakeholders who have low power to influence an NPO's operation, yet they have direct impact on the beneficiaries, the NPO should keep them engaged and updated about its mission and strategic agenda. They could be external service providers with professional knowledge whom the NPO has outsourced the service to. For instance, Lion Befrienders collaborated with Active SG to develop exercise regimes for seniors. The exercises can be conducted both at the elderly care centres or by volunteers when they visit seniors at their homes. Although this type of collaboration could be short-term involving knowledge transfer, the NPO may keep the stakeholders engaged, educate them about the its mission and strategy, so that subsequently, there will be more opportunities for collaboration.

4.4.3.4 *Low power to influence X indirect impact on beneficiaries*

The last category of stakeholder, the one with lower power to influence an NPO's operation and indirect impact on the beneficiaries, may be the capability builders that NPO engages with externally, such as technology providers, transportation or logistic providers, or corporate donors. A possible engagement strategy would be for the NPO to keep them informed and help them to understand the core mission of the NPO and its beneficiaries, so that there could be opportunities for them to become more involved.

Exhibit 4.6 outlines the steps to prepare for engaging stakeholders. Once the NPO determines an engagement strategy for the

Exhibit 4.6: Steps to Prepare for Engaging Stakeholders

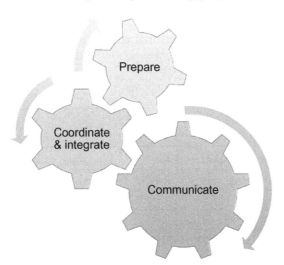

stakeholder group, they can prepare to engage with stakeholders with the process outlined in Exhibit 4.6. These steps are not independent from one another, but can be used in conjunction with one another.

4.4.3.5 *Preparation to engage*

To engage with stakeholders, NPOs and their managers need to establish a set of internal organisational processes in preparation. The preparation work includes identifying and analysing stakeholders, and determining the underlying demands and priorities of the stakeholders. Finding this information may require NPO managers to use social networks, media or internet searches, and environmental scanning. Leaders and managers will conduct internal discussions to determine how to engage, whom to engage, and who would represent the NPO to engage with the stakeholder. The outcome of this internal discussion is a stakeholder management plan so that other organisational members can discuss and follow. Exhibit 4.7 tabulates a sample stakeholder management plan.

4.4.3.6 *Coordination and integration*

Once a stakeholder management plan is established, the NPO should coordinate the action plan, determine who will engage with the stakeholder, the channel and level of engagement. This decision will be based on the level of organisational resources the NPO has, and the

Exhibit 4.7: A Sample of Stakeholder Management Plan

Stakeholder group/name	Engagement action	Point of contact	Channel	Frequency
Volunteer/Brian	Collaborate	Sam	WhatsApp, email, f2f	Weekly
Trainer/Tina	Keep engaged	Evelyn	Whatsapp, email	Monthly

stakeholders' expectations and demands. Some important decisions for the course of action include:

- Do we engage with this stakeholder group directly or indirectly?
- What part of the stakeholder's demand can we fulfil completely, accommodate, defer, or outsource?
- Can we negotiate with the stakeholder, on what basis?
- Do we need to come up with any new solution or programmes to address the stakeholder's demand?

It is also possible that managers use a combination of the afore-mentioned strategies to engage with the stakeholder and prioritise stakeholders according to their salience.

4.4.3.7 *Communication*

We now turn to a key step of stakeholder management, which is communication. The key to communication is perspective-taking, meaning that the speaker is taking the perspective of the listeners and see their situations from their organisational lens (Parker & Axtell, 2001).

For instance, an NPO manager, Mark, wants to engage with student volunteers for an event, and Mark is responsible to communicate with the school representatives, including administrators and teachers, and solicit their interests to participate in the event. But the school's administrator and teachers will also have to communicate with the students' parents to receive their consent for allowing students to participate in a charity event. Therefore, teachers and parents of the students become the NPO's indirect stakeholders who will influence students' interest and participation.

To communicate effectively with the school's representative, Mark has to take their perspective, understand the situations, concerns, and even potential problems they may face when communicating the event with the parents. Mark has to consider what kind of information the school would need to convince the parents. The more thoughtful Mark is when considering the school–parent relation, the better he can provide the relevant information and reduce the barrier for the school and parents. This is what we called perspective-taking.

Perspective-taking is more than empathy where the speaker feels the emotion of the listener; a cognitive process occurs as where the speaker observes and makes sense of the listener's organisational contexts and interests as they communicate with each other. Adopting perspective-taking will bring the speaker to change the mindset from "what I want" to "how can I help".

4.4.4 *How to Engage and Monitor the Stakeholder Continuously?*

The last question to consider for stakeholder management is: How should NPOs engage and monitor stakeholders continuously? As stakeholder management should be a part of an NPO's routine and planning, NPO leaders and managers should also reflect on the organisation's mission statement and purpose, and assess how well stakeholder relations enable its mission, or whether its stakeholder strategies reflect its values.

Stakeholder positions, interests, and priorities could change, or their expectations could become different over time; NPO's organisational resources could also change. Therefore, an evaluation process needs to be in place on a regular basis to check whether progress is made and whether the engagement strategies remain relevant (Preble, 2005).

Ask yourself the following questions:

- Towards powerful and legitimate stakeholders: "Am I accumulating enough managerial capability to respond to them?"
- Towards my beneficiaries: "Am I fulfilling their needs? Am I closer to achieving the mission?"
- Towards volunteers: "Am I clear with conveying my mission," "Am I providing them enough organisational support," and "Do my volunteers understand my organisational culture and are they committed to my mission?"

Through internal discussion and reflection, managers will be able to develop a set of indicators or signs that reflect stakeholder relations. The discussion and reflection can be documented not only for executing the stakeholder management plan, but also to accumulate knowledge and foster an organisational environment conducive to learning (see Chapter 5 for more).

4.5 Conclusion

In conclusion, this chapter discusses the concepts and processes involved in conducting stakeholder analysis in order to manage different types of stakeholders effectively. Stakeholders are critical for NPOs to fulfil their social missions, as no NPO can have all the resources and capabilities itself; engaging and partnering with stakeholders is a strategic choice and requires discipline. Stakeholder management begins with knowing who they are, and identifying what is at stake for them, in order to develop the appropriate engagement strategy. Successful stakeholder management also requires managers to inspire stakeholders about the NPO's mission and become willing to participate, and thus communication is critical. Stakeholder management can become a capability and be a part of the organisational culture, so that the NPO will eventually become more embedded in the greater ecosystem.

References

DiMaggio, P. J., & Powell, W. W. (1983). The iron cage revisited: Institutional isomorphism and collective rationality in organisational fields. *American Sociological Review, 48*(2), 147–160.

Freeman, R. E. (2010). *Strategic Management: A Stakeholder Approach.* Cambridge University Press.

Mitchell, R. K., Agle, B. R., & Wood, D. J. (1997). Toward a theory of stakeholder identification and salience: Defining the principle of who and what really counts. *Academy of Management Review, 22*(4), 853–886.

Parker, S. K., & Axtell, C. M. (2001). Seeing another viewpoint: Antecedents and outcomes of employee perspective taking. *Academy of Management Journal, 44*(6), 1085–1100.

Preble, J. F. (2005). Toward a comprehensive model of stakeholder management. *Business and Society Review, 110*(4), 407–431.

Chapter 5

Transforming into a Learning Organisation

5.1 Introduction

This chapter builds on the previous chapters about organisation character and stakeholder management to discuss leadership and learning organisations. The focus of this chapter is on human capital development such as in developing employees in non-profit organisations (NPOs) through learning as opposed to mere investments in training. A disciplined strategy to human capital development entails expanding beyond knowledge, skills, and attitudes to include reflection, team learning, and organisational learning.

What is a Learning Organisation? Senge (1990) defined a learning organisation as one in which people are continually expanding their capacity to create results they truly desire, where new and expansive patterns of thinking are nurtured, collective aspirations are set free, and where people are continually learning to learn together.

5.2 Why a Learning Non-Profit Organisation?

The importance of learning to an organisation can be viewed from three perspectives: the individual, team, and organisational levels, and its operating environment. An NPO operates in a complex environment; the needs of beneficiaries are multidimensional and stakeholders bring with them diverse expectations and requirements. Therefore, NPOs must be able to learn continuously and sense-make to stay relevant and contribute effectively and efficiently to the community.

Sense-making is a process that assigns meaning to new information; we attach meaning to new information when we emplace new information in our prior knowledge or mental schema (Weick, 1995). Taking a leaf from military organisations that operate in highly complex, volatile, and uncertain environments, for example, the US Army embarked on the journey of transformation with a strong emphasis on learning, following the unsatisfactory results of the Vietnam War. To learn, the US Army reflected on and adjusted their assumptions and methods.[1]

Systems were developed and built for training to simulate real combat. Beyond the realistic simulation and scenario-based learning, specific focus was placed on the development of competence, spirit, and confidence of every man in the force. Leaders in the US Army also used on-the-ground action as the crucible for learning.

Today, this practice is one of the best and longest running models of emergent learning. They named it the "after action review" (AAR). More of the AAR will be discussed in the later part of the chapter (Parry & Darling, 2001).

Another example is the regular but concise case discussions in healthcare organisations. Typically a multidisciplinary team of doctors, nurses, physiotherapists, social workers, and administrators convene to discuss complex patient cases and identify strategies to overcome physiological, psychological, and social issues they observed that patients, caregivers, and their families are grappling with (Taberna *et al.*, 2020).

In the commercial world, many Japanese firms handle learning in a routine but effective way. For example, the CEO of a highly successful retail chain personally reviews and responds to feedback logged by employees who work in the retail stores distributed all over Japan. Staff including temporary staff are required to log their observations and feedback of the store that they operate in. On a daily basis, the CEO reads the lengthy spreadsheet of operational issues that the store manager records and responds to each one religiously through direct delegation to his next level executive or empowering action on the

---

[1] https://hbr.org/2005/07/learning-in-the-thick-of-it

ground. This is an example of learning from the most senior to the most junior in the organisation.

Today, many organisations including NPOs use social media platforms like Facebook Workplace to connect virtually and to keep up with both operational issues as well as internal communication. Learning can happen through communication when there is reflection from action, and action that follows from the reflection could advance both individuals and teams.

An NPO relies on employees and volunteers to serve the primary beneficiaries. Thus, for the NPO to be effective in living its purpose and mission, developing people — employees and volunteers — has to be a core focus.

There is a general misconception that learning is about sending staff for more training and courses. While attending training and courses is essential for learning new knowledge and skills, it is only one form of structured learning. Training or structured learning is effective only when there is a transfer of knowledge and skills to the job. Besides learning takes place each day in our tasks and activities at work as an individual and collectively in teams and groups. Leaders and managers are responsible to design the workplace for unstructured learning to occur and for the transfer of knowledge and skills gained through structured learning to performance.

More often than not, the employees and volunteers of an NPO possess rich and diverse knowledge and skills. Their emotional connection to the NPO's social mission can be harnessed if we could introduce a consistent learning strategy into the workplace for teams and people development. Workplace learning as a strategy could be framed as part of an organisation's capability development for staff retention. Workplace learning can also be a strategy to attract prospective employees who are intrinsically motivated, those who seek growth for future employees who are looking for growth opportunities, meaning, and purpose as top priority in their career choice (Billett, 1995).

The traditional linear approach of study–work–retire is fast becoming irrelevant in a rapidly changing and connected work environment. In the past, one attended school to learn, join the "real world" to work, and then retire. Now unlearn, learn, and relearn are common phrases that we hear to stay relevant in the workplace. Lifelong learning is not just a buzzword but an essential mental model that embraces learning throughout our lives in order to adapt and stay abreast of the changing world.

These perspectives from an organisation and its operating context, the team, and individual levels are impetuses for NPOs to embark on the transformation into learning organisations.

5.3 What are the Characteristics of a Learning Non-Profit Organisation?

Staff and leaders of the NPO enjoy and adopt a growth mindset. They actively participate in the learning process and seek out opportunities to derive joy for learning from every programme and daily encounter. Their learning is centred on the values and purpose of the NPO.

The organisational values guide our motivation to acquire deeper knowledge and skills to serving its purpose and mission. When staff can see the alignment and orientation towards the purpose, learning will be more efficient, effective, and joyful. This alignment of purpose and values are especially important for adult learners.

Leaders and managers could support their staff to connect the dots to the strategic goal, appreciate the value of learning, and create a supportive environment to apply their learning.

5.4 What are Challenges Faced by a Learning Non-Profit Organisation?

The challenge of a learning NPO is to develop people to embrace creativity, deal with complexity, and collaborate with others to serve the beneficiaries and the community.

5.4.1 Embrace Creativity

In the cause of work, staff and leaders have to manage many individual beneficiary cases. While there is a Standard Operating Procedure (SOP), there is no textbook solution because each case and every beneficiary is unique. Thinking out-of-the-box is necessary to support beneficiaries in overcoming their problems.

Understanding the methodology of problem-solving is not sufficient. We also need to learn to understand the "whys?" behind the issue. Resources are always limited. Learning, reframing, and embracing creativity to unlock the constraints are critical.

For example, the Aravind Eye Hospital[2] employs a "McDonald's" concept of process standardisation to increase its throughput of eye surgery. This standardisation unlocked the constraint on a key asset — eye doctors. Aravind Eye Hospital reframed their purpose to be a training school and supported the learning and practicum of trainee doctors under the supervision of qualified doctors. As the trainee doctors conducted more eye procedures, their skills and proficiency level improved. By reframing from a key constraint to possibility, Aravind Eye Hospital is able to support the patient demands. Besides, many local females from the rural areas were recruited and trained as nurses and assistants to conduct checks for patients and prepare them for the eye procedures. Designed in this way, the standardisation optimised the human capital — doctors do what only doctor can do, while employment opportunities were created for women in rural villages.

5.4.2 *Dealing with Complexity*

In the NPO, it is not easy to deal with the complex, dynamic, and multifaceted issues that each beneficiary or client is grappling with. To determine what is important and what are the relevant causal and contributory factors, we require different sources of information. This demands from us deep learning and examination.

This ability to appreciate diverse perspectives and hold the tension among them for decision-making is the hallmark of a wise leader. This is easier said than done.

For example, a family staying in a rental flat was once functional but became dysfunctional with a series of life episodes and interlocking issues. The vicious cycle started when the father quit his work to take care of his wife who had her limbs amputated due to diabetics.

---

[2] https://aravind.org.

Due to the unrelenting demands, the father suffered a minor stroke and the daughter who is married had to leave her job to take care of both parents. This added to the financial burden. The stress and tension consequently led to the dissolution of her marriage that in turn affected her school-going kids emotionally and psychologically. Her children started to play truant and their academic performance suffered.

To support the family, we need to look beyond individuals and silos, to learn the interdependencies and provide a more holistic scaffolding to see the family through these life challenges.

5.4.3 *Collaborate with Others*

Beyond individual learning, team learning is important for staff to work, learn, and serve collectively as one. Staff needs an environment to learn to cooperate and coordinate with one another to serve and strive for excellence. Taking it to the organisation level, collaboration across organisations is built on the respective organisational strengths. Additionally, each organisation must learn to be flexible to realise synergy that will benefit its clients and community.

5.5 Digitisation, Digitalisation, and Digital Transformation

Digitisation, digitalisation, and digital transformation are different concepts. Digitisation refers to information; digitisation converts information in physical form into digital format. Digitalisation refers to processes; digitalisation turns operational processes using software technology to drive operations. Digital transformation incorporates digitisation and digitalisation to scale up operations and expand the organisational scope.

Thus, digital transformation does not happen overnight by definition. However digital transformation is necessary to stay abreast in a volatile, uncertain, complex, and ambiguous (VUCA) world.

The point of leverage in digital transformation is change management, in response to internal resistance to change. However, taking the transformation journey in short, quick, and effective successions can help to build the momentum for the transformation journey. The digital transformation example of the Food from the Heart NPO illustrates think big, start small, scale fast.

To better serve their beneficiaries, Food from the Heart has been ramping up its digitalisation processes in the past few years: from food distribution operations to volunteer-assignment systems to fundraising platforms, and a new food donation management system. Food from the Heart moved away from manual tracking to seamless barcode scanning capability in the warehouse in quick succession. The change enhanced the volunteers' experience since the volunteers were deployed to sort donated food items in the warehouse. Efficiency improved as the processes were streamlined when 70% of work was cut away; instead of manual forms, volunteers now use barcode scanners to record the food items into the inventory.[3]

5.6 Learning Disabilities of Organisations

Learning disabilities can paralyse individuals and organisations. Senge (1990) identified four learning disabilities.

5.6.1 *First, I am My Position*

It is not uncommon to hear a colleague or sometimes even ourselves as leaders and managers declare that "I am just a case manager," or "I am just a nurse or social worker," and lament that, "I cannot do this and that" to emphasise the self-limiting influence of our roles.

While we cannot choose the stimulus or the situation, we can certainly choose our perspective and response. For every role we assume, we can choose our response no matter how overwhelming

---

[3] https://www.foodfromtheheart.sg/highlights/using-technology-to-give-better-improving-food-donation-management-system-108.

the dynamics can be. Likewise, we can adopt our desired mental model and reframe our perspectives to be relevant to the context.

5.6.2 *Second, the Enemy is Out There*

When a problem arises, the instinct is to point the blame on others: the client, caregivers, community, and the government agencies; everyone else except ourselves. This "externalisation" of blame is unhealthy for learning. We need to reframe this "victim" paradigm and reflect on how we can take charge and do something about the problem.

5.6.3 *Third, the Myth of Management Team*

Beyond blaming someone else for the problem, we are also guilty of the mindset that the problem lies in the board or the audit committee. We assume that the management team will deal with the problem.

This myth that the management team can and will resolve everything, is not uncommon. The reality is no one knows our job better than ourselves. Instead of relying on the management, we should learn to take charge and proactively resolve our problems where we can.

5.6.4 *Last, It is the Parable of the Boiled Frog*

When placed into a pot of boiling water, a frog will jump straight out of it. If the same frog is placed in a pot of water and you increase the water temperature gradually, the frog will adapt to changes in the water temperature until it is boiled.

Our behaviour mimics the boiling frog in this parable; we would continuously adapt to our circumstances until the day we are faced with a crisis at the workplace. From reactive and adaptive actions, we need to consider adopting more reflective and generative paradigms to perceive and resolve problems with a higher leverage point — a smaller amount of change force can cause a large change in system behaviour.

Exhibit 5.1: Self, Team, and Organisational Learning

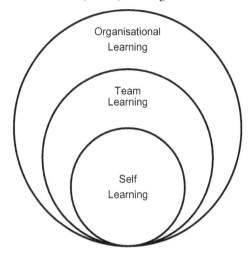

5.7 Self, Team, and Organisational Learning

As a leader of an NPO, how do I start to build a learning organisation? We take the three levels approach — from self to team and then organisational level learning, to discuss the salient processes and considerations at each level. Exhibit 5.1 is a diagrammatic representation of self, team, and organisational learning.

5.7.1 *Level 1: Self-Learning*

A leader is first a learner. It is important for a leader to be a self-directed learner who takes ownership of one's learning needs and goals. Being a self-directed learner also means one takes an independent approach to be engaged in the learning process (Knowles, 1975).

Self-reflection heightens one's awareness of one's most effective learning strategy. Thus, a leader should engage in reflection.

As leaders in the NPOs, we are pre-occupied with the multiple operational tasks we handle. A reflective leader would set aside time to examine his/her actions and judgement in his/her work. As a reflective leader, s/he teleports him-/herself back mentally into past situations at work to re-examine from different perspectives.

Such mental processes enable us to gain insights and enrich our knowledge. As leaders, we could engage in discussions with our colleagues and gain insights from their perspectives on completed projects or everyday tasks and activities. These reflections should be written down as the process of writing allows us to re-visit our thoughts and build on our knowledge. Leaders and managers of learning organisations instil such reflective activities as daily team routine.

5.7.2 *How Do We Practise Self-Reflection?*

Take deliberate actions to set aside time to pause, find a quiet place to think back on past situations, especially the challenging circumstances. We can ask ourselves some guiding questions:

- Why did we do what we were doing?
- Is this the best way to do what we were doing?
- Are there alternate and better ways of achieving the same outcomes?

The focus is not to form answers to these questions. The value behind reflection is the discipline of leaders to step back and get out of the daily grind of back-to-back meetings to re-focus on the meaning of our work. The aim is for an alignment of our values, mission, and vision in relation to our everyday activities. Through this regular reflective practice, our experiences are processed and translated into learning.

At the workshops for the COC-SUSS Certificate in High Performing Charities conducted by the Singapore University of Social Sciences (SUSS), participants including board volunteers, leaders, and managers from charities, Institutions of Public Character, social enterprises, public agencies, and commercial entities are encouraged to reflect deeply on their learning, experiences from work, and class discussions. The self-reflection that is facilitated aims to assimilate the habits of reflection in these leaders. From the commencement of the course since 2019 to date, the students have shown a depth of thinking and generated insights that are evident from their reflection pieces. Some of the past participants' reflection pieces are as follows.

5.7.2.1 *Excerpt 1 — Self-reflections on volunteer management by Dr Lily Yeo (March 2021)*

What is the one key thing I learnt today about volunteer management?
Motivations behind why people volunteer: UVSPEC, which stands for Understanding, Value adding, Social responsibility, Protectionism, Enhancement, and as a Career. For those who volunteer with the intention of decorating the CV, I sincerely hope that they will find the true meaning behind it all and continue to contribute to do good.

Also, how we promote better collaborations with the volunteers: SCARF, or Status, Certainty, Autonomy, Relatedness, and Fairness

What is my charity's one major pain point regarding volunteer management?
What I learnt from the workshop will be to attract and retain volunteers to stay committed.

What can I learn about seeing this pain point as a possibility?
To create a better sense of community, through closer peer support with knitted integration of the employees and volunteers and the environment conducive to building a trusting relationship to achieve the common goals.

What is the one key thing I can put in place to achieve alignment between staff and volunteers in my charity?
Fulfillment of needs is the key here. I can relate well to one participant's comments that as an organisation, we need to progress and the practices are likely to change in order to stay relevant. It is important to have open discussions with volunteers to ensure alignment of their personal causes with the organisation's. I believe all volunteers want to do good and contribute, and hence it is important for the volunteer management to prepare the volunteers for the transformation

process, to better understand why changes are needed to stay relevant and garner their support, so that both the personal and organisation's needs are able to be fulfilled together.

What have the members of my learning circle taught me about volunteer management?
The comment from another participant made an impression. He challenged the introduction of technology (Chatbot) would remove the personal touch, in particular when we are dealing with clients who were potentially at high risk. While we are looking into improving the efficiency of internal processes to better serve the community, it is important we continue to be outward looking, and not lose touch, as the welfare of our beneficiaries should remain the top focus. This ties back with what we learnt in Workshop 1, 不忘初心 — translated to "staying true to our mission" or "not to forget our initial passion of the cause".

5.7.2.2 *Excerpt 2 — Self-reflection on fundraising by Ms Foo Kok Wan (March 2021)*

What is a key idea about fundraising?
I learnt that our charity's brand name is crucial. We must be able to communicate our identity clearly to potential stakeholders. We must show good leadership, governance, excellent volunteer management, and have easy-to-grasp fundraising models.

What is my charity's core brand value?
It is important to know our core brand value to align with our donor's motivations. We have identified that our core brand value is producing original productions and staging a major show every year.

What is my charity's fundraising model(s)?
Our fundraising model appeals to successful individuals, corporations, or foundations who support the traditional performing arts. We aim to receive personal donations from individuals and financial support or collaborative tie-ups from corporations' CSR departments and grants from foundations. We must gain their trust in our authenticity as preservers of our cultural heritage to pass on this legacy for the future.

How will I align my charity's brand value to our donors' motivations? Name one action.
Our donors are passionate about keeping traditions alive and passing on the legacy to the next generation. We will get their support as long as we aspire to be a premium arts organisation producing good original shows every year. A case in point is finding the successful entrepreneur to be a patron. He is a Nantah alumnus who cherishes preserving the Chinese language and culture.

The participants' sharing of their personal reflections gave us a pause on what we ourselves have done. Example, at times when we perceived that we are doing something different, we coined cliché terms like "innovation" and "breakthrough". But on close examination, we were merely doing the same thing in a different manner.

If we want to achieve a true breakthrough, we need to commit ourselves as leaders to reflect and be self-directed learners.

5.7.3 *Level 2: Team Learning*

Team is the fundamental unit of an organisation. Team learning increases collective intelligence of the team which exceeds the sum of intelligence of its individual members (Senge, 1990). Team learning unleashes the collective power of every member in the team.

Team learning is about synergy. It is like a football team. Everyone has a role in the game, be it a captain, attacker, defender, midfielder, or a goalkeeper. Every role is important to the team. A team that harnesses the strengths of everyone, learns together and inspires the team spirit, enables the team to stay in the game. To achieve this team synergy, collective power is needed.

5.7.4 *Core Theory of Success*

The core theory of success states that an increase in the quality of relationships leads to an increase in the quality of thinking, which in turn improves the quality of actions and the quality of results. The increase in the quality of results will lead to better quality of relationships and the loop is self-reinforcing (Kim, 1997).

Exhibit 5.2: Core Theory of Success

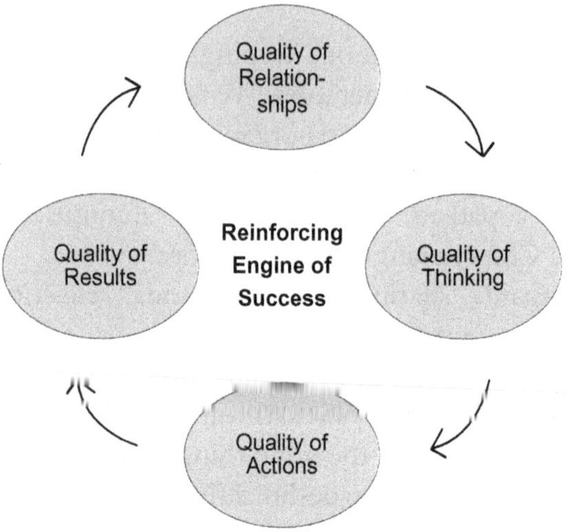

Source: Adapted from https://thesystemsthinker.com/what-is-your-organizations-core-theory-of-success/.

Team learning enhances trust and relational quality by building mutual understanding and quality of conversations. Exhibit 5.2 illustrates the core theory of success.

5.7.4.1 *Why is quality of conversation essential to team learning?*

Leadership is the ability to make an influence. To make an influence, a leader begins with having conversations. Team learning involves collective communication, thinking, and actions.

To learn effectively as a team, open communication is essential. For the team to speak their hearts and minds, the team must feel psychologically safe. In a quality of conversation, there is a free flow of dialogue, a balance between inquiry (asking) and advocacy (telling), and members listen deeply to one another (Bohm, 1990). A team gains insights when conversations contain inquiry and advocacy; inquiry demonstrates curiosity, and advocacy lends clarity. Exhibit 5.3 is a diagrammatic representation of the quality of conversation.

Exhibit 5.3: Quality of Conversation

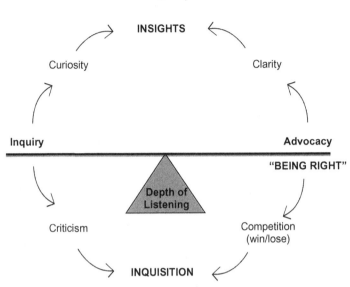

Source: Adapted from http://www.sdibaonline.org/Presentations/Cournoyer.pdf.

On the contrary, if inquiry is expressed with a tone of criticism and advocacy is orientated towards competition, the conversation leads to inquisition or interrogation (Bohm, 1990).

To achieve a psychological safety and quality of conversation, the leader can garner the commitment of the team to establish a common set of guidelines. An example of conversational guidelines is as follows:

- Speak openly and freely;
- Listen with heart and mind;
- Ask to seek clarity;
- Suspend judgement;
- Respect the views of others.

5.7.4.2 *How do I promote quality of conversations to support team learning?*

There are three simple tools to help promote quality of conversations in your workplace:

- Check in/Check out Process;
- After Action Review;
- Open Space Technology.

Please see the detailed process of the tools in Appendix A.

5.7.5 Ladder of Inference

5.7.5.1 How do we understand what drives our beliefs and actions — mental models?

Ladder of inference is a framework to describe how people form mental models (Argyris, 1982). Our world views are shaped by the way we view reality, make assumptions in our lives, and respond to problems (Senge, 1990). We must acknowledge that our assumptions can be wrong, especially when we make assumptions about the intentions and beliefs of others. Re-examining our mental models leads to new perceived reality, which can change our actions. Exhibit 5.4 presents an example of a ladder of inference.

Exhibit 5.4:   Ladder of Inference

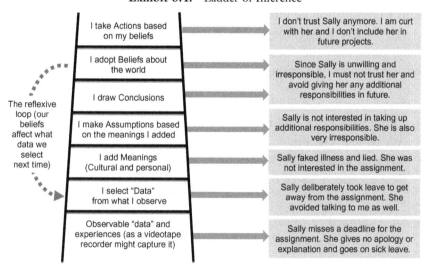

Source: Adapted from Senge (1990).

We experience and collect data with our senses — our eyes and ears. We select the data that we feel are relevant. We add meaning to the selected data based on our cultural and personal experiences. We then make assumptions to make the perceived reality complete and draw conclusions with this perceived reality. We adopt the conclusion as our belief. We act on the belief as if it were a proven fact.

As we adopt a belief and form our mental models, we develop "tunnel vision" to select the data that further reinforces this belief. This belief also filters other data and restricts the perception of opportunities and stifles creativity. This is also known as the reflexive loop.

Different mental models will drive different actions. For example, a patient-centric perspective of dementia care often focuses on the best care for the clients with dementia. This assumes the best for the client. A caregiver-centric perspective will consider the caregiver of persons with dementia who form the support system. A caregiver-centric model adopts both the client and support system perspectives to deliver a more holistic care.[4]

5.7.6 *Learning — Practice — Reflection — Reframing*

5.7.6.1 *What are single- and double-loop learning?*

In a single-loop learning, we focus on the strategies, actions, and performance outcomes. We match the results against the desired outcomes to identify performance variance. In this way, we "re-act" to the processes without any major adjustment to the primary design, goals, and assumptions (Argyris, 1976).

A common example of single-loop learning is the thermostat that regulates the temperature of a boiler. The thermostat will turn off the boiler when the temperature of the water reaches the desired level and turns on again when temperature drops to the pre-set level.

Problem-solving and improving the system are common modes of operations in an organisation. Single-loop learning is a simple process. It deals with the strategies and techniques, and clarifies the actions and results, obtaining the results and resolving what was done right

---

[4] https://www.channelnewsasia.com/author/11666240.

while highlighting areas to improve. In short, when the process enables the organisation to carry on its present policies or achieve its objectives, it may be called single-loop learning.

An example is the Meals-on-Wheels, meal delivery programme[5] which is designed to meet the daily meal needs of the home-bound elderly. An elderly, who lives alone, depends on the volunteers of Meals-on-Wheels to deliver their meals every day. The programme is designed to fulfil the needs of the elderly through meals delivery — single-loop learning.

6.7.7 Double-Loop Learning

In double-loop learning, we go beyond fixing the problem, to clarify our assumptions, values, and beliefs. We correct the deviation in desired outcomes by changing the rules. This mode of learning requires us to reflect and think outside the box. Double-loop learning focuses on why we do what we do. Through double-loop learning, we can create strategies and techniques, and uncover the assumptions behind the results.

An example of double-loop learning can be gleaned from the following excerpt for the meals delivery programme[6]:

> Reports indicated that while the intentions were good, the programme sometimes fell short of meeting needs. A total of 125 organisations such as soup kitchens and Meals-On-Wheels are involved in this food support. Study found that more than half of the 44 severely food-insecure households interviewed had infrequent or no food support at all and others reported that some households received multiple packets of meals — which suggested inefficiencies in the charitable food support eco-system.

One assumption to be validated is the match between the quality of meals provided and the beneficiary's needs. For example, are the

---

[5] https://www.touch.org.sg/get-involved/volunteer/details/meals-on-wheels-2021.

[6] https://www.channelnewsasia.com/news/cnainsider/food-insecurity-hunger-singapore-charity-donations-taskforce-12460350.

meals appropriate for those with health conditions like diabetes, or those with dietary requirements due to their religion, such as Halal food for the Muslims?

The nutritional needs of beneficiaries may be complex and guidelines that are too broad, fail to address different and unique individual needs. While logistically challenging, the approach has to be more personalised. For example, many charities distribute dry rations such as rice, canned food, and high sugar sachet beverages to seniors during festive periods. The rations with high sugar and salt content are unsuitable for seniors suffering from diabetes and hypertension. In addition, some elderly beneficiaries suffer from arthritis and they struggle to open Milo tins. In such instances, other packaging like sachet-form drink mixes would serve them better.

As discussed, double-loop learning calls for us to reflect from the results we obtained and dig deeper to validate our assumptions. The strategies and techniques could then be refined to match the desired outcomes. Exhibit 5.5 illustrates the concepts of single- and double-loop learning.

5.7.8 *Reframing the Model of Service*

The following examples demonstrate the criticality of learning, reflection, and reframing to challenge our assumptions and reimagine new models to serve our beneficiaries better.

Exhibit 5.5: Single- and Double-Loop Learning

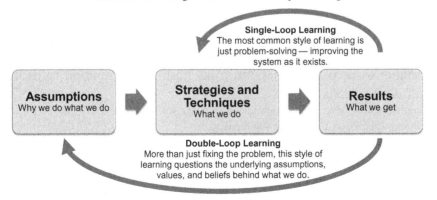

Source: Adapted from https://orl9.wordpress.com/single-and-double-loop-learning/.

The Loving Heart[7] is located in Jurong East. To provide hot meals to the disadvantaged in the area, Loving Heart coordinated with the stall owners of coffee shops and hawker centres. Loving Heart distributed food vouchers to their beneficiaries which they can use in exchange for hot meals. This reframing gives beneficiaries the autonomy over their choice of food. Moreover, the beneficiaries are obliged to get out of their homes; this incidentally provides opportunity for human interactions and physical activity. This model promotes neighbourliness and instils the kampung spirit to look out for one another. The social capital built will go a long way in creating a caring and cohesive community.

Another reframing example is The Food Bank's food pantry,[8] which has been reimagined as convenient 24-hour vending machines[9] that provide emergency rations and meals to beneficiaries in Toa Payoh. The beneficiaries receive cash cards that are topped up with 50 credits which they can "buy" or exchange for 25 items each month. The purpose is to make food more accessible any time they need it — empowering the beneficiaries with choice.

The third example involves SG Food Rescue (SGFR)[10] — which collects unsellable fresh produce from suppliers at Pasir Panjang Wholesale Centre and other places — which has been redistributing excess fresh produce to partners, welfare homes, and charities. It has also been stocking free-for-all community fridges, which are open 24/7 at seven locations. Vegetables and fruits are definitely more nutritious than instant noodles. This model gives people better options by tapping into the tonnes of food waste to feed the food insecure.

While this idea is gathering momentum in Singapore, it is not without its challenges. Most charities and groups lack chilled storage facilities to keep vegetables and fruits fresh for distribution to their

---

[7] Source: The Loving Heart (www.lovingheart.org.sg).
[8] Source: The Food Bank (www.foodbank.sg).
[9] Source: Channel NewsAsia (https://www.channelnewsasia.com/watch/disadvantaged-toa-payoh-families-benefit-charity-food-vending-machine-video-1492826).
[10] Source: SG Food Rescue (sgfoodrescue.wordpress.com).

primary beneficiaries nor do they have the requisite manpower and resources to process and deliver these perishables in a timely manner.

5.7.9 *Level 3: Organisational Learning*

Organisational learning is a process of creating and transferring knowledge within an organisation. Learning can take place at the individual, team, organisational, as well as inter-organisational levels. Beyond standard training programmes, organisational learning aims to develop and grow a learning culture within the NPO. A learning culture builds trust, drives engagement, deepens relationships, and supports shared vision for continuous learning and improvement.

There are two processes that are useful to support organisational learning among NPOs: building Communities of Practice (CoP) and workplace learning.

The notion of CoPs has been around for 25 years in professional practice and everyday language (Wenger, 2010). CoPs refer to groups of people who genuinely care about the same real-life problems and interact regularly to learn together and from each other (Wenger *et al.*, 2002).

NPOs and their diverse stakeholders can come together to create CoPs to share best practices and brainstorm to solve problems collectively. Collective learning facilitates the shortening of learning curves among partners who face similar challenges. Collective learning also supports systemic change from deeper collaboration. CoPs can be further established for both internal staff and external partners. Interactions from CoPs build trust and relationships, further promoting collective thinking and actions.

In the COC-SUSS's Certificate in High Performing Charities course, executive participants from diverse NPOs and sectors are organised into learning circles for the programme that stretches over 5 weeks. The intent is to develop CoPs so that the participants can continue to collaborate and share their learning after graduating from the course.

A few of these learning circles have emerged into CoPs. For example, Tzu Chi Humanistic Youth Centre in Yishun has inked their collaboration with Silver Ribbon to train the Tzu Chi volunteers on mental wellness and self-care. Silver Ribbon counsellors also conduct regular counselling sessions for youth at the Centre. Alzheimer Disease Association and Bizlink Centre signed a Memorandum of Understanding (MOU) to further their collaboration. Hopefully, we can see more charities coming together to build CoPs to share, learn, and serve as one.

5.7.10 Workplace Learning

Leaders and managers can use the workplace to offer an abundance of learning opportunities or set constraints that regulate employee participation and learning (Billett, 2004).

The workplace offers a rich learning environment for individuals and teams. Workplace learning strategy involves making learning deliberate, systematic, and comprehensive for continual improvement of the individuals and organisations. Each of us as a leader and an employee learns daily at work.

Public agencies and private companies are encouraged to put in place progressive workplace learning practices to build capabilities and strengthen core competencies. NPOs should consider working with agencies such as the National Centre of Excellence (NACE) led by Nanyang Polytechnic and Institute of Adult Learning's (IAL) Centre for Workplace Learning and Performance, to embark on workplace learning strategy.[11]

5.8 Conclusion

A learning NPO is one where learning is core and central to its being. The leaders are reflective and the employees are engaged through learning. The employees are self-directed learners and teamwork is

---

[11] Source: *The Straits Times* (https://www.straitstimes.com/singapore/new-national-certification-scheme-to-help-local-firms-close-workplace-learning-gaps).

strengthened through quality conversations. Employees feel psychologically safe to speak their minds and hearts. Both leaders and employees feel connected and engaged in their daily work and change management.

Learning can be joyful and meaningful. Learning that is anchored on the values, purpose, and vision of the organisation is meaningful and purposeful. Learning takes place at the individual, team, and organisational levels.

Learning and application are integrated. Through CoPs and workplace learning, learning becomes systematic, comprehensive, and deliberate. Collective thinking and actions happen when learning is central to the NPO.

References

Argyris, C. (1976). Single-loop and double-loop models in research on decision making. *Administrative Science Quarterly*, 21(3), 363–375.

Argyris, C. (1982). The executive mind and double-loop learning. *Organizational dynamics*, 11(2), 5–22.

Billett, S. (1995). *Workplace Learning: Its Potential and Limitations. Education + Training*. Emerald Insight.

Billett, S. (2004). Workplace participatory practices: Conceptualising workplaces as learning environments. *Journal of Workplace Learning*, 16(6), 312–324.

Bohm, D. (1990). *On Dialogue*. David Bohm Seminars.

Kim, D. (1997). What is your organisation's core theory of success. *The Systems Thinker*, 8(3), 1–5.

Knowles, M. S. (1975). *Self-Directed Learning: A Guide for Learners and Teachers*.

Parry, C. S., & Darling, M. J. (2001). Emergent learning in action: The after action review. *The Systems Thinker*, 12(8), 1–5.

Senge, P. (1990). The fifth discipline: The art & practice of learning organization. *Currency*. New York.

Taberna, M., Gil Moncayo, F., Jané-Salas, E., Antonio, M., Arribas, L., Vilajosana, E., Torres, E. P., & Mesía, R. (2020). The multidisciplinary team (MDT) approach and quality of care. *Frontiers in Oncology*, 10, 85.

Weick, K. E. (1995). *Sensemaking in Organizations* (Vol. 3). Sage.

Wenger, E. (2010). Communities of Practice and social learning systems: The career of a concept. In: Blackmore, C. (ed.) *Social Learning Systems and Communities of Practice* (pp. 179–198). London: Springer Verlag and the Open University.

Wenger, E., McDermott, R., & Snyder, W. M. (2002). *Cultivating Communities of Practice*. Boston, MA: Harvard Business School Press.

Chapter 6
Driving Social Performance

6.1 Introduction

Between financial performance and social performance, I find the former relatively easier to manage and achieve. Unlike social performance, the financial performance of an organisation falls within the control of managers who are privy to internal data and measures. On the other hand, social performance includes environmental factors that fall outside the span of managerial control. Additionally, organisations can attain financial performance with short-term tactics like headcount cuts and asset disposal. Such tactics, however, cannot be applied to social performance, which evaluates the effect of change due to an organisation's actions on communities and societies. The impact on communities and societies are outside the control of the organisation. Moreover, social performance takes time to manifest.

Non-profit organisations (NPOs), including charity organisations, typically operate in a complex ecosystem with diverse stakeholder expectations. To be effective, non-profit leaders must implement the management discipline and rigour to manage and drive social performance.

The purpose of this chapter is to discuss the management concepts and frameworks that an NPO can employ in the drive for social performance. We focus on the organisational underpinnings to measure social performance instead of social impact, drawing on the performance frameworks like the logic model, theory of change, social return on investment (ROI), and social enterprise balanced scorecard.

6.2 Define Social Performance

Founded in 1969, the Samaritans of Singapore (SOS) provides an available lifeline to anyone in crisis (www.sos.org.sg). SOS aims to address the needs of persons in crisis through its 24-by-7 hotline, offering a listening ear to callers to reduce unnecessary deaths by suicide through crisis intervention as well as a combination of prevention and post-intervention programmes and services like outreach and bereavement support for suicide survivors

Social performance aggregates the inputs and activities to deliver intended outcomes aligned with the particular NPO or charity's social mission. Given the social mission of SOS, which is to be the available lifeline to anyone in crisis, the intended outcome would be to reduce unwanted deaths caused by suicide.

The word "social" in "social performance" refers to the non-economic outcomes that improve the lives of people, communities, and the wider society. The social performance of NPOs refers to the value created for individuals and the community-at-large that are consistent with an NPO's mission and purpose. The measurement for social performance should therefore complement the existing strategy of the NPO.

In the example above, the target beneficiaries of SOS are persons in crisis. NPOs, including charity organisations, exist to address the market gap observed in the community or broader society for a target group of beneficiaries whose needs have not been addressed by the private and public sectors. However, there may be other reasons for existence.

In Singapore, some charities are appointed to conduct programmes and services following a set of requirements and standards to a target beneficiary segment defined by the government agencies. These NPOs tend to draw a significant portion of their funding from government grants and subvention. Examples are residential services for adults with disabilities and nursing homes for the elderly. The social performance of such non-profit entities would refer to its effectiveness in achieving the mission, purpose, and goals aligned with government requirements and standards.

6.2.1 *Social Impact*

Social impact falls under the domain of social performance. Social impact measures the sustained positive change in people's lives at the societal or ecosystem level. Social impact manifests over time and is the result of achieving the defined social outcomes.

Following this definition, the social impact for SOS would be a sustained and significant reduction in suicide deaths. In Singapore, our public housing policy has made a social impact — providing home ownership to the masses and eliminating squatters.

Social impact addresses the root cause(s) of the social problem using a system's lens. By taking a system's lens, social impact is outward-looking, impacting others instead of the organisation like financial performance. The social impact extends beyond organisational boundaries to deliver social change in collaboration with extra-organisational actors or external stakeholders.

Social impact is a sustained, significant, and systemic change at the ecosystem level. Hence by definition, social impact is rarely achieved by one organisation single-handedly.

For example, the goal to reduce or eliminate needless preventable suicide deaths in modern Singapore calls for the collaboration of multiple organisations across people, private, and public sectors who are aligned around a shared set of desired outcomes. The strategy should include various sectors, including the local communities and the media. The effort of one single entity is insufficient. Moreover, only time will tell if the performance is sustained.

6.2.2 *Your Organisation's Theory of Change*

The drive for social performance begins with your NPO's theory of change, your organisation's desired social change. A theory typically identifies a relationship between two phenomena. A theory of change can be defined as the change or changes that result from the NPO's intervention. Exhibit 6.1 shows a diagrammatic representation of a theory of change.

Exhibit 6.1:   Theory of Change

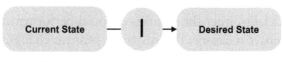

I = *Intervention*

Ebrahim (2019) refers to a theory of change as "a causal logic", a series of "if-then" statements that articulate how a particular organisation's interventions address the social problem to achieve expected outcomes. This interpretation encompasses both the what (i.e., social goal and outcome) and the how (i.e., intervention).

The change(s) in the theory of change can occur at different levels — individual, group, community, societal, ecosystem, population-wide. At the societal level, how is the society and its culture affected by your NPO's mission? At the individual level, what are the effects of your programmes and services on the primary beneficiaries? The types of changes can be economic, financial, physical, behavioural, psychological, emotional, cultural, and/or social processes.

As a recommendation, build your organisational theory of change based on formal research evidence instead of a tacit understanding of social norms.

One example of formal research would be the scientific evidence of the safety and efficacy of oral polio vaccine for infants and young children against poliomyelitis; the widespread introduction of mRNA COVID-19 vaccine and reduced incidence of SARS-CoV-2 in a population as a means to controlling infection rates in a population. The advocacy and promotion of at least 150-minute per week in moderate-intensity physical activity both recreational and non-recreational is grounded in scientific evidence for its inverse relationship with cardiovascular disease (DeFina *et al.*, 2019; Higueras-Fresnillo *et al.*, 2018; Koba *et al.*, 2011; Kwon *et al.*, 2020; Lear *et al.*, 2017; Lee *et al.*, 2016; Nocon *et al.*, 2008; O'Donovan *et al.*, 2017; Zhao *et al.*, 2020).

An example of one based on tacit understanding of social norms would be the broad consensus that access to education leads to improved living standards and overall well-being. Take the "Youth for

Good" initiative by TikTok of ByteDance to teach young people to create educational content with the video-sharing app and support peers with mental health issues.[1] Through the training, the targeted change is improved peer support for mental health issues and online well-being.

Wherever possible, you should build your NPO's theory of change on formal research to establish the causal link between your activities (or programmes and services) and outcomes. A theory of change specifies the cause–effect relationship between an intervention and the expected outcomes.

A logic model enables you to translate the theory of change into practical measures for monitoring and evaluation. The logic model clarifies how your organisation implements the theory of change.

6.2.3 *Logic Model*

A logic model, also known as a pipeline logic, or impact map, diagrammatically represents the "how" or the causal pathway through which activities can be expected to lead to outcomes. The logic model is a linear pipeline of inputs, activities or processes, outputs, outcomes and impact. Exhibit 6.2 illustrates a logic model to improve the well-being of isolated seniors through meals delivery and befriending.

Using the logic model, we can derive the appropriate process measures and indicators for monitoring progress and effects, organisational learning, and strategic reflection.

The visual representation allows the logic model to drive organisational alignment and communicate a coherent organisational strategy for the theory of change. The model provides clarity of thinking in the intervention and the associated output and outcome measures.

---

[1] *Source*: *The Straits Times* (access: https://www.straitstimes.com/singapore/tiktok-to-work-with-government-local-non-profits-to-train-youths-to-become-mental-health#:~:text=The%20programme%20aims%20to%20teach,said%20TikTok%20in%20a%20statement.&text=They%20also%20spoke%20on%20the,speaking%20up%20about%20mental%20health.).

Exhibit 6.2: Mapping the Logic Model of Meals Delivery and Befriending

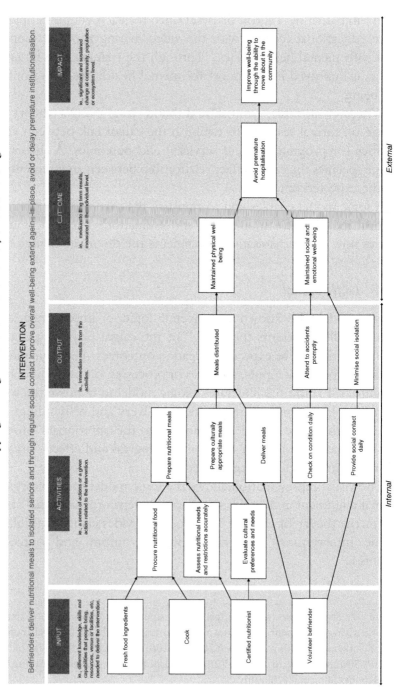

Outputs, outcomes, and impact are assumed to be resultant from inputs and activities. Like a flowchart, you begin with a set of inputs related to the intervention, programme or initiative. The inputs needed to deliver the intervention refer to different knowledge, skills, and capabilities that people bring with them, financial resources like fees, technology hardware and software, venue or facilities, and so on. Activities refer to a series of actions or a given action related to the intervention. Outputs refer to the immediate results from the activities. Output is a form of process measure from inputs to activities. In the example provided on meals delivery, outputs include the number of meals eaten, the number of accidents attended to promptly, and the number of social isolations minimised.

Outcomes are the medium to long-term results and are measured at the individual level. Outcomes are the effects of inputs, activities, and outputs. An intermediate or medium-term outcome for the intervention designed to benefit isolated seniors can be maintaining physical, social, and emotional well-being. Such individual-level outcomes can be measured using clinically validated scales or observed through behavioural traits. A longer-term outcome would be the avoidance of premature hospitalisation as a result of accidents at home.

Outputs are distinct from outcomes. Outputs are short-term results that arise from inputs and activities. An output measure reports results within the organisation like the number of meals distributed and consumed as shown in Exhibit 6.2. Although mapped linearly in the logic model, outputs do not necessarily lead to outcomes. A higher number of meals consumed does not necessarily translate to improved physical well-being. Likewise, individual outcomes do not always lead to societal outcomes.

As another example, in their bid to eliminate needless blindness, Aravind Eye Hospital has performed over 306,000 cataract surgeries, screened more than 563,000 persons for conditions like diabetic retinopathy, glaucoma, refractive errors, and retinopathy of prematurity in the financial year ending 31 March 2019.[2] The number of

---

[2] *Source*: Aravind Eye Care System Annual report 2018–2019 (access: https://aravind.org/wp-content/uploads/2020/07/Activity-Report_2018-19.pdf).

cataract surgeries, number of people screened, and number of visions regained are output measures. An individual outcome would be the mobility gained, his/her subsequent employment, and improved living conditions with economic employment. The related impact from Aravind's mission is poverty reduction (Ebrahim & Rangan, 2014) with gainful employment and economic progress. Yet, there are many contributing factors to one's sustained employment, not to mention collective, sustained employment to achieve poverty reduction and economic progress in the population.

Impact refers to the results that are measured at group level such as communities, society, population, or ecosystem. Impact reflects a change in the root cause and is significant, systemic, and sustained over time.

6.3 Performance Beyond Organisational Boundaries

Take the example of a frailty prevention programme "Share a Pot" introduced by a geriatrician at Khoo Teck Puat Hospital. The input components of the logic model include raw ingredients for preparing the pot of soup, equipment, devices for monitoring functional abilities, venue for conducting the project, and skills for the fitness activity. These inputs translate to activities including cooking, exercises, and functional assessment. The outputs would be number of seniors participating in the project, number of sites, number of seniors retained, number of newly recruited seniors, and number of pots consumed.

The outcomes in this instance would refer to benefits at the individual and community levels. There can be intermediate or medium-term and ultimate or longer-term outcomes from the programme goals that you can define. Some intermediate individual outcomes may include an increase in the number of friends or social network and physical activity. The ultimate long-term outcome is an improvement in gait and balance, fitness, or reduction in frailty score. A natural extension of impact here is the seniors' health and well-being, which can be measured by better control over chronic conditions, lower risks of premature hospitalisation, and lower hospitalisation costs. Please map the logic model using the information and template provided in Appendix B.

Suppose the seniors who participated in the programme grew their social network and their physical activity improved based on the number of steps monitored, can we attribute the improvement to the programme? How certain are we that these seniors could maintain their health and fitness level to avoid premature institutionalisation and hospitalisation? The intervention introduced by the programme is not an isolated event but a part of the daily living activities of the seniors. The association between cause (i.e., intervention) and effect (i.e., increase in physical activity) is uncertain and can be attributed to other factors.

Along the logic chain from input, output, and outcome to impact, an organisation's control over the results of each chain reduces from left to right. A particular NPO has better control over results at input and output. This is because the perspective is inward within the organisation. At the outcome and impact chains of the model, the perspective shifts outside the organisation to measure improvements made to individual beneficiaries, communities, society, or the ecosystem. Hence, the organisation's control over results to be delivered at the outcome level is reduced, significantly more so at the systems level for social impact.

A social change model considers the NPO's intervention within the wider social context, also known as system framing (Ebrahim, 2019). Using a system framing, we can assess the organisation's intervention in a broader social context.

Other daily routines and social activities interfere with one's participation in the "Share a Pot" programme. These factors that are external to the programme affect the desired outcome of frailty prevention.

Take another example of a family service centre. A family service centre serves persons in the lower-income strata and disadvantaged families to improve their economic stability and overall well-being.[3]

---

[3] *Source*: Ministry of Social & Family Development (access: https://www.msf.gov.sg/policies/Strong-and-Stable-Families/Supporting-Families/Pages/Family-Service-Centres.aspx).

Each family service centre is part of the wider ecosystem of social service agencies, educational, health, and healthcare institutions trying to improve the quality of life of marginalised individuals.

Social performance thus requires the collaboration of different stakeholder participants across the for-profit, non-profit, and public sectors to bring about desired goals, outcomes, and social change.

6.4 Systems Framing and Social Change

According to the World Health Organization, one suicide occurs every 40 seconds around the world and 39% of all suicides occur in the Southeast Asia Region (Vijayakumar *et al.*, 2020). In Singapore, the Immigration and Checkpoint Authority reported the highest incidence of suicide among those aged 10–29 in 2018 since 1991.[4]

More recently, the SOS reported 452 suicides in 2020 including a rise in suicide deaths among the elderly compared to 2019.[5] This works out to be more than one suicide death daily here. A significant and sustainable reduction in needless death by suicide would be a social impact. Recall our earlier interpretation of social impact as one that addresses the root cause(s) of the social problem.

The interventions and complementary changes are required at the upstream, midstream (or in-stream), and downstream to effectively tackle root causes.

The analogy is that of many people drowning in a fast-flowing and dangerous stream (Eagle *et al.*, 2013). To rescue and revive drowning people, those on land are deployed to dive into the stream for the mission. If people are frequently falling into the stream, it would be more effective to go upstream to tackle the root cause, such as to erect a barrier that will prevent people from falling into the dangerous stream.

At the upstream, the priority is on prevention by addressing the determinants of social problems through contextual and

---

[4] *Source*: ICA Singapore (access: https://www.ica.gov.sg/docs/default-source/ica/stats/annual-bd-statistics/stats_2018_annual_rbd_report.pdf).
[5] *Source*: *The Straits Times* (access: https://www.straitstimes.com/singapore/452-suicides-reported-in-singapore-in-2020-amid-covid-19-highest-since-2012).

environmental factors such as legislation, policy formulation, and prioritisation, that may encourage, detract, or be an obstacle to desired social change. As an example, research evidence suggests an association between suicide and social isolation (Trout, 1980; Voracek, 2007). Consequently, an upstream intervention related to mental well-being could be the shaping of a caring and connected community, in person and the virtual world, allocating budget to influence strategies that will make families stronger.

At the midstream, when the problem has occurred, the focus is on the individual or community level, helping people cope with and improve their ability to handle the situation and threats to well-being. In the example of SOS, the accessibility and availability of crisis-intervention hotlines and specialist counselling for persons in distress are examples of midstream intervention.

Downstream intervention focuses on the deployment of tactical interventions that will influence a specific individual or group behaviours. An example in the context of suicide prevention is in the form of grief and bereavement support for suicide survivors. For every death by suicide, five to six individuals are affected by the traumatic loss. These suicide survivors may be family members, friends, and related persons.

A comprehensive system frame to address the problem upstream, midstream, and downstream is necessary for social impact.

6.5 Social Impact Assessment versus Programme Evaluation

Social impact assessment and programme evaluation are distinct concepts. The latter relates to the goal of a specific intervention centred on upstream prevention, intervention at midstream or downstream post-vention. In other words, social impact assesses change that occurs system-wide, while programme evaluation tends to focus on the evaluation at the sub-system level.

Drawing reference to the ecological context of health behaviours (Sallis *et al.*, 2006) that was built on Bronfenbrenner's ecological

Exhibit 6.3: Hierarchy of Influence on an Individual Adapted from Bronfenbrenner's Ecological Systems Theory

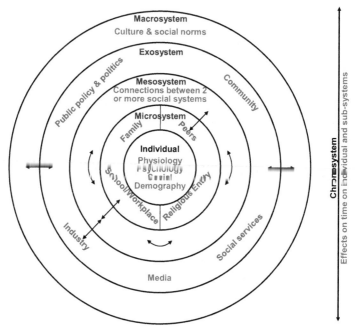

systems theory,[6] an individual resides at the core of an "onion" or a layered structure that comprises the microsystem, mesosystem, exo-system, macrosystem, and chronosystem. Exhibit 6.3 shows the hier-archy of influence on an individual adapted from the ecological systems theory.

Notice that the sub-systems represent the hierarchy of influence on the individual's cognition and behaviours. The microsystem refers to the environmental system with direct impact on the individual, e.g., family, school, peers. The outermost layer is the macrosystem of values, attitudes, culture, social norms, and beliefs that permeate the micro-, meso-, and exo-system. The sub-systems interact and evolve

---

[6] *Source*: Ecological systems theory (https://en.wikipedia.org/wiki/Ecological_systems_theory).

with time (i.e., chronosystem) to influence an individual over the life course. Social impact occurs at the macrosystem layer.

6.5.1 *A Complex Web of Direct and Indirect Effects*

Take the example of a 24-by-7 crisis intervention helpline, the evaluation of this programme intervention is likely output-centred, including the number of calls answered, calls abandoned, calls assessed with suicide risks, and calls escalated for professional follow-up.

One life lost to suicide is one too many. Therefore, such a helpline plays an invaluable role in our community. While these are output measures, the function of the helpline is significant to arrest the vicious cycle of depressive self-deprecating thoughts that can lead to a suicide attempt. Yet, a single entity alone is not enough to achieve a sustained reduction in suicide rates in the population or system-wide. Besides, there is a high degree of uncertainty to isolate the effects of the helpline to a community-wide sustained and significant drop in suicide rates.

Take another example of a NPO that trains caregivers of persons with dementia. The training programme is the intervention, and the programme's evaluation may include the number of caregivers trained and trainees' satisfaction of learning outcomes.

By social impact, we aim for lasting and significant positive change in the society, not only productivity measures, efficiency indicators, or individual-level outcomes. Instead, there is often the need to align multiple interventions or programmes against a shared set of desired outcomes by the NPO and other organisations outside the non-profit sector to produce a positive impact. In the case of caregiver training, a measure of individual outcome would be caregiver health and well-being.

The reality is often far more complex than the diagrammatic representation of a linear logic model or impact map. While the impact map looks like a linear sequence or pipeline of chains, social impact is not the logical outcome of social programmes and services, although the programme outcomes can contribute to social performance and social impact. For example, addressing the well-being of community-dwelling seniors is complex (like the meals delivery and befriending example in Exhibit 6.2), not one that can be achieved with only nutritious meals and social support. The causal link is more like a web of direct and indirect effects than a linear sequence of driver and consequence.

6.5.2 Sustainability Development Goals

The 17 sustainability development goals (SDGs) that have been defined by the United Nations (https://sdgs.un.org/goals) are a set of goals under the 2030 Agenda for Sustainability Development (2030 Agenda). These goals are exemplars of what social impact can look like.

The 17 SDGs range from poverty elimination, quality education, responsible consumption, and production, to climate action. Collectively the goals are built on the premise that our economy, society, and environment are interconnected. Hence, the 17th sustainability goal call for partnerships across sectors to realise these national goals. Co-led by the Ministry of Foreign Affairs and the Ministry of Sustainability and the Environment, Singapore supports the 2030 Agenda.[7] The 2018 Voluntary National Review report was presented to the UN High-Level Political Forum to report on the nation's domestic and international progress and efforts on sustainability development.

For the 17 SDGs, the United Nations established 169 targets and 247 associated indicators to measure progress towards the targets. For example, the description of SDG 3 is about good health and well-being. Related to SDG 3, target 3.4 states, "By 2030, reduce by one-third premature mortality from non-communicable diseases through prevention and treatment and promote mental health and well-being." Cardiovascular disease, cancer, diabetes, and chronic respiratory disease are the four primary causes of non-communicable diseases that are a burden across populations. Related to target 3.4, the indicator 3.4.1 is expressed as: "Mortality rate attributed to cardiovascular disease, cancer, diabetes or chronic respiratory disease."

---

[7] *Source*: SingStat Website page on SDGs (access: https://www.singstat.gov.sg/find-data/sdg).

Reducing the risk of premature mortality from such diseases is a worthy target that would contribute to good health. However, realising this target calls for a collective commitment of various organisations and an orchestrated strategy with different and diverse stakeholder participants. Therefore, the United Nations promotes and advocates multilateralism and broad ownership to implement these goals.

Social change can happen when NPOs focus on their desired social performance and account for their chosen output and outcomes aligned with their mission. Social performance is contingent on the NPO's chosen organisation strategy and working collaboratively with other stakeholder participants on shared goals.

6.6 Social Balanced Scorecard

The logic model concisely mapped the chain from inputs to outcomes and the impact of an NPO's espoused theory of change. The associated measures and indicators can be stated at each chain to monitor progress. Nevertheless, the logic model does not capture the NPO's strategy to achieve the desired outcome and impact. Consequently, the logic model does not elucidate the extra-organisational partnerships or stakeholders necessary for system-level change. The social enterprise balanced scorecard and ecosystem strategy map make up for these deficiencies in the logic model.

The balanced scorecard (Kaplan & Norton, 1996) has broad appeal in business organisations as a performance management tool articulating performance measurement and organisational strategy. This tool links individual and organisational learning and growth to supporting structures that will ultimately deliver value to customers and achieve the business's financial goals. Using the balanced scorecard, the organisational strategy is made visible to internal stakeholders as the causal linkages are mapped; intangible assets like people, information, and customer relationships are mapped to tangible outcomes like profit margins and market share. Furthermore, the tool indicates the accompanying objectives, measures, targets, and initiatives against the goals. Exhibit 6.4 shows a balanced scorecard adapted for non-profits (Kaplan, 2001).

Exhibit 6.4: The Balanced Scorecard Adapted to NPCs

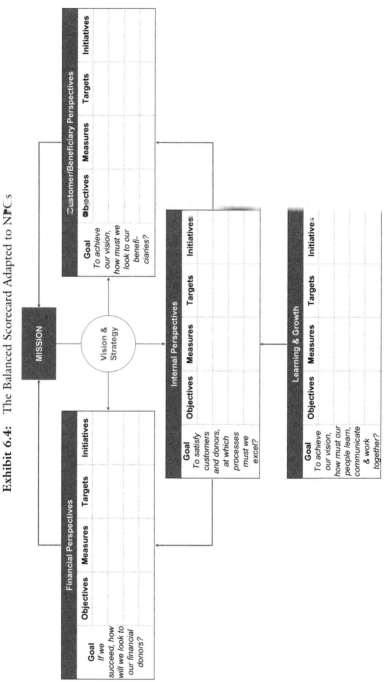

Customer/Beneficiary Perspectives			
Objectives	**Measures**	**Targets**	**Initiatives**
Goal *To achieve our vision, how must we look to our beneficiaries?*			

Internal Perspectives			
Objectives	**Measures**	**Targets**	**Initiatives**
Goal *To satisfy customers and donors, at which processes must we excel?*			

Learning & Growth			
Objectives	**Measures**	**Targets**	**Initiatives**
Goal *To achieve our vision, how must our people learn, communicate & work together?*			

Financial Perspectives			
Objectives	**Measures**	**Targets**	**Initiatives**
Goal *If we succeed, how will we look to our financial donors?*			

MISSION

Vision & Strategy

Source: Kaplan (2001).

Exhibit 6.5: Social Enterprise Balanced Scorecard

State Social Goal (Desired Outcomes)
Financial Sustainability Perspective e.g., increase financial resources, manage costs
Stakeholder Perspective e.g., funders, beneficiaries, employees, grassroots, partners
Internal Process Perspective e.g., internal processes, information sharing, impact measurement, internal & external communications
Resources Perspective e.g., technology, knowledge & skills, social networks

Source: Somers (2005).

The social enterprise balanced scorecard (Somers, 2005) is another adaptation of the classic balanced scorecard to articulate the strategy of an NPO's intended social goal. Exhibit 6.5 describes the four different dimensions of a social enterprise balanced scorecard. Analogous to the logic model, the social enterprise balanced scorecard maps the causal links from the resource enablers to the desired outcomes. Instead of inputs and activities, the social enterprise balanced scorecard refers to them as "resources" or "key enablers and resources".

The key enablers and resources in a social performance system are often not confined to those internal to the NPO, i.e., intra-organisation. They may include partnerships with multiple external stakeholders like complementary organisations, donors, and funders (please refer to Chapter 2). With extra-organisational collaboration, a system of sustainable and innovative processes (Kaplan & McMillan, 2020) is designed and implemented to realise value for different stakeholder participants. These extra-organisational processes substitute the internal processes in the classic, balanced scorecard. Kaplan and McMillan (2020) called this the ecosystem strategy map.

Exhibit 6.6:   Social Balanced Scorecard Adapted from Social Enterprise Scorecard and Ecosystem Strategy Map

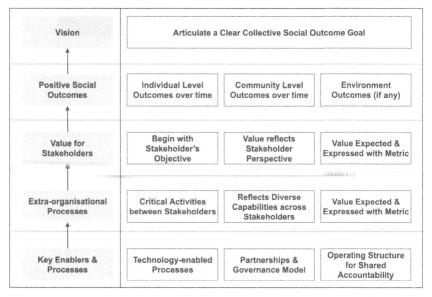

Value in a balanced scorecard must be expressed from the perspectives of different stakeholders. In the example of meals delivery and befriending, value for the seniors is access to nutritious meals and more regular social interaction; value for volunteers is increased sense of fulfilment and community strength from their ongoing participation in the programme; value to the healthcare system is a lower cost of subsidised care when the risk of premature hospitalisation is decreased.

Exhibit 6.6 presents a template adapted from the social enterprise balanced scorecard devised in the UK as well as the ecosystem strategy map.

Consider the social balanced scorecard as your organisational visual aid for performance management when your organisational strategy for social change requires the participation of external stakeholders. Such a scorecard enables you to communicate a collective value creation process.

6.6.1 *Four Types of Social Change Strategy*

As a strategy, your organisation must choose between output or outcome measures, attribution or contribution to the desired social change and between a singular focused strategy or a portfolio strategy that combines different interventions jointly with a constellation of partners.

In his book, *Measuring Social Change: Performance and Accountability in a Complex World*, Ebrahim (2019) presented four types of strategies for social change; each strategy is contingent on two dimensions. The first refers to the organisation's theory of change or the articulated causal pathway leading to desired social change. The second dimension is the organisational control over outcomes. The four types of social change strategies are: niche, integrated, emergent, and ecosystem. Exhibit 6.7 shows the contingency framework for social performance.

A niche strategy requires standardisation to produce reliable outputs. An integrated strategy prioritises the combination of multiple outputs to produce the desired outcome. Emergent strategy is suitable for organisations that operate in rapidly changing settings with little control over outcomes and low certainty over cause–effect of action and outcome. The fourth type of social change strategy is termed an ecosystem strategy. The operating context is complex and nonlinear in which the cause–effect logic is weak, and no single actor can independently produce the desired outcomes. One such example is the reduction of the recidivism rate. Along the chain from the penal system, crime prevention to incarceration, rehabilitation, and community integration, multiple organisations are involved in achieving the desired social outcome. An ecosystem strategy orchestrates the actions of these organisations by coordinating the tasks and decision-making towards a collective outcome most appropriate to achieving a lasting and significant drop in recidivism.

The contingency framework for social change strategy underscores the importance of understanding the ecosystem or environmental context that the NPO is operating in. Your strategic choice

Exhibit 6.7: A Contingency Framework for Social Performance

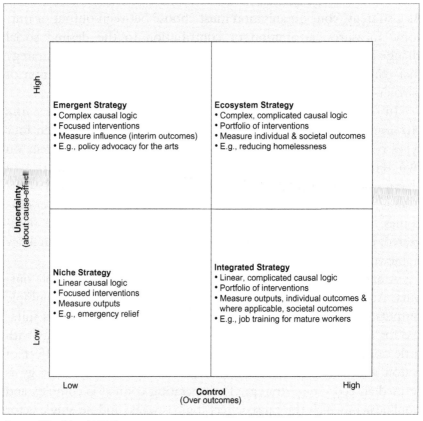

Source: Ebrahim (2019).

defines your performance management and measurement system. Suppose the strategic choice for your NPO is a niche strategy from the evaluation of the ecosystem, your NPO can be both productive and effective by focusing on operational standardisation to produce reliable and high-quality outputs rather than expending resources to build capabilities and capacities to measure outcomes.

6.7 Quantifying Social Performance

In reality, NPOs are under pressure to comply and report specific metrics to attract funding or possible donations from prospective funders, donors or grantmakers. The demands from funders and donors can be at odds with the organisation mission and purpose. Moreover, given the trend towards structured giving, donors and funders are increasingly asking for evidence to demonstrate the utility of their donations or prospective donations.

The philosophy and social movement that draw on evidence and reasoning to determine the most effective ways to benefit others is coined "effective altruism" by Singer (2015). Donors who are effective altruists want to evaluate what is the most good for the same or similar cause, given the value of the gift. In such a situation, the organisations should have clarity on their operating costs and quantify the benefits that they are delivering to the primary beneficiaries and what they can reasonably deliver given their existing capabilities and capacities.

At Singer's website "The Life You Can Save" (https://www.thelifeyoucansave.org/) named after his book, he presents a list of charities that have been evaluated to assure donors of the maximum impact for their donation dollars. Given your choice of charity and gift value, you can calculate the impact of your donation on your chosen charity. For example, a gift valued at US$1,000 to Evidence Action can deworm 2,000 children from an estimated 280 million children in Africa and Asia who are at risk of parasitic worms from unsafe water.

The above is one method for charities to demonstrate impact. There are various methods to quantify social performance evaluation that would demonstrate how a particular NPO brings about social change. Effectiveness matters because a majority of NPOs desires to bring about lasting solutions to social problems, and these NPOs should have the management and leadership know-how to be financially sustainable to realise their desired social change.

Many social performance measures are adapted from private and public organisational settings, including grantmakers, using the financial accounting principles and the common decision-making language. Among them are included the social ROI, benefit-cost ratios, and economic rate of return. Others include subjective well-being as well as qualitative measures. Appendix C compiles some common performance measurement methods and relevant resources. In the following, we discuss the social ROI or SROI.

ROI or financial ROI is the net present value of accumulated returns or cash flow from an investment against the investment. Unlike the financial ROI, social ROI can be complicated. SROI was first articulated by the San Francisco's Roberts Enterprise Development Fund (REDF) in 2000.[8] The REDF is a philanthropic fund that makes long-term grants to organisations that operate in the business for social benefits.

SROI creates a single ROI number that includes both a financial and a social ROI. The formula for SROI is present value against the value of inputs; present value is obtained from the proxies assigned to intangible value. The sequence of a logic model forms the foundation in computing the SROI as all inputs, outputs, and outcomes are expressed and quantified in monetary terms to arrive at the equivalent present value for the cost items and desired outcomes.

Doran and Kinchan (2020) quantify the economic and epidemio-logical impact of youth suicide by measuring the impact for 10 countries with the highest human development index according to the United Nations Human Development Programme.[9] Using figures from 2014, adjusted GDP per capita, growth rates, and real interest rates, the average cost of suicide, the research reported 3,078 total years of life lost from suicide in Singapore, the average cost of suicide is estimated at $1,747,170, and the present value of lost earning potential from youth suicide is a staggering $85,383,942 in 2014 international dollars. Using an economic value expressed by the present value of lost earning potential due to youth suicide quantifies the magnitude of adverse outcomes with suicide and the potential benefits explicitly to be realised by investing in addressing suicide risks and behaviours.

---

[8] *Source*: Roberts Enterprise Development Fund (access: https://redf.org/).
[9] *Source*: UN Development Programme — Human Development Report 2016 (access: http://hdr.undp.org/sites/default/files/2016_human_development_report.pdf).

Another example is the value of training persons with special needs for employable skills. In such instances, the financial returns could be quantified using the projected income stream, the desired employment outcome over an approximate duration of employment, and the likelihood of employment for the group of trainees.

Before computing the net present value, you first need to find or even fund systematic research to quantify your organisational intervention; translate the desired outcomes and impacts into economic or financial terms. Due to the assumptions inherent in the inquiry process, the computation of SROI can be both time and resource consuming. However, there are benefits in deliberating the assumptions as the process encourages communication and engagement with internal and external stakeholder participants. For example, SROI can facilitate the board of directors of a charity to better allocate resources for different programmes and services.

By deliberating who will be affected by your intervention and how you are creating value, both you and your stakeholders gain clarity over your organisational strategic goals and objectives. Quantitative measures offer a systematic and common reference point to align perspectives and negotiate when perspectives differ, or motivation and interests deviate.

Many who have had experience working in both for-profit and non-profit sectors would agree that performance management is more straightforward in a for-profit organisation — the quantifiable financial performance goal lends a sharp and non-negotiable objective. The clarity of the endgame forms the baseline for consistent monitoring and continuous improvement. The same can be adopted in NPO performance reporting. An objective, quantifiable measure integrated with the disbursement of additional grants to the NPO can be a robust motivational tool.

Just like there is no one golden metric to capture the social value created, the SROI also does not convey any change in individual or community outcomes, quality of life, and well-being. Hence, before your NPO embarks on any SROI exercise, it is vital that your organisation clarifies the purpose, and acknowledges your internal capabilities and capacities to sustain the measure over time in a consistent fashion.

6.8 Qualitative Evaluation for Social Change

The nature of social performance, like human services, makes it hard to distil performance into objective and explicit quantitative measures. Take the example of subjective well-being. This self-reported measure of individual well-being has multiple iterations, and psychologists prefer multifaceted test batteries that include components like cognition, personality, and emotion to assessing subjective well-being (Diener, 2009). Meanwhile, there is yet one universally accepted definition and measurement for subjective well-being at the community, society, or national levels. For a holistic assessment of social performance, combine quantitative and qualitative approaches to report performance outcomes.

The implication here is to place as much emphasis on formally documenting outcomes from the perspective of the NPO's primary beneficiaries and stakeholder participants, including staff involved and engaged in the intervention. Qualitative reports are standard in news writing. Qualitative reports promote awareness and help different stakeholders connect with the particular charity organisation's mission and purpose.

Funders, donors, and policymakers can make better sense of the NPO's role in the community from their performance narratives. Human interest stories that narrate why a particular NPO matters to the lives of beneficiaries are invaluable for internal and external stakeholder communication.

Interviews may be conducted with primary and secondary beneficiaries, staff, and critical stakeholder participants. Such stories remind donors and philanthropists of their motivation for supporting your NPO's cause. Besides, only the NPO is in the position to seek out the cooperation of the beneficiaries to tell their stories, their struggles, and how the community can be better through the change that the NPO is trying to make.

These stories should also be integrated with your public outreach and advocacy initiatives to help external stakeholders and members of the public appreciate the plight of your NPO's primary beneficiaries. Irrespective, there is a general distrust over qualitative measures because of small sample sizes and the manner in which respondents are recruited. Attribution bias as such applies regardless of qualitative or quantitative measures. So, pay attention to assure integrity in data collection and formulate your data governance principles.

The other forms of qualitative performance evaluation can be stakeholder feedback from interviews, narratives from documentary analysis and observations. Appendix C further tabulates several examples and resources for qualitative reporting measures.

Another example of qualitative reporting is in the format of exhibits and galleries. Tzu Chi Foundation in Singapore opened the Da Ai Gallery in Sembawang.[10] The Gallery is a thoughtfully curated space that showcases the deeds, "humanistic culture", and values of Tzu Chi Foundation. The exhibits in the Gallery are deliberately organised using different artefacts symbolic of Tzu Chi's mission to tell stories through the perspectives of beneficiaries and Tzu Chi's founder, Master Cheng Yen. This concrete testament of Tzu Chi's teachings and charity work through the Gallery galvanises visitors to Tzu Chi's diverse missions from bone marrow donation, charity, community volunteerism, education, environmental protection, humanistic culture, international relief to medicine.

6.9 Design a System to Drive Social Performance

In the earlier chapter on "Transforming into a Learning Organisation", we introduced single- and double-loop learning. A performance system devises appropriate strategies and tactics to deliver the organisation's desired results. The strategy and tactics are contingent on or draw from your organisational capabilities and capacities.

---

[10] *Source*: Tzu Chi Foundation (access: https://www.tzuchi.org.sg/en/our-missions/humanistic-culture/da-ai-gallery/).

To be the leading university for social good, the strategies that the Singapore University of Social Sciences deploys towards its vision are centred on research and education in social sciences. Whereas the strategy for a bank with its vision to be a force for good will likely centre on responsible financing and financial inclusion.

The design of a performance system in the drive for social performance should consider the required processes, technology, and available financial and human resources that would shape and sustain a robust, rigorous, and respected measurement process and system. For example, setting up a database to record activities and output measures will require a data governance framework to guide consistency in data capture. Setting up a data governance framework is onerous but a necessary investment because if done well, you gain trust from your internal stakeholders. And if executed well, you only need to do it once, and there will be integrity in knowledge transfer.

The measures to monitor social performance can be referenced from your logic model or social enterprise balanced scorecard. These indicators and measurements should be holistic, comprising both quantitative and qualitative indicators. Take the logic model of meals delivery and befriending, you can determine the indicators and measures like the example provided in Exhibit 6.2.

A well-designed performance system can support your drive for social performance through the twin engines of strategic reflection (recall organisation learning discussed in Chapter 5) and communication.

First and foremost, it is a system for strategic reflection. A reflection on progress towards your desired outcomes; the intended and unintended consequences of your intervention; net social benefits namely, deadweight, displacement, attribution effects; factors that contributed to performance and underperformance; the need for new resources and capabilities internally and externally; the relevance of your outcomes against widespread system changes.

An effective performance system incorporates single- and double-loop learning. Single-loop learning addresses the problems and issues in strategies when results fall short, reviewing the tactics and processes for areas of improvement. In double-loop learning, the performance results give pause for strategic reflection — to validate assumptions and beliefs of your organisation's strategies. Beyond tackling the operations, processes, and activities, assumptions are reframed and strategies refined to attain the desired outcome.

Using the example of meals delivery, when isolated seniors remain nutritionally deficient despite the meals distributed, one of the problems identified may include the size of the meal portion, i.e., too small. Single-loop learning that could fix the problem may increase the portion size. A double-loop system digs deep to reflect on the assumptions that may lead to dietary constraints, e.g., meals are unsuitable for seniors with chronic conditions like Type 2 diabetes. Instead of increasing portion size, it would be more appropriate to distribute meals suitable for seniors with underlying pathologies like diabetes. Additionally, displacement effects occur when seniors with Type 2 diabetes consume delivered meals high in processed sugar. This unintended consequence displaces the health outcomes of any diabetic medication that the seniors are consuming.

A performance system is a system of continuous learning to realise the desired short-, medium-, and long-term outcomes. An effective performance system serves as a regular and independent validation of the particular NPO's relevance on the broader society and a monitoring tool in view of the NPO's interdependence with other actors in the ecosystem who share the desired long-term outcome.

In the example of meals delivery, the desired long-term outcome is reduced risks of premature hospitalisation among isolated seniors (recall the example in Exhibit 6.2). A dominant actor in the ecosystem who shares the similar desired outcome is the Agency for Integrated Care (AIC), responsible to oversee, coordinate, and facilitate all efforts in care integration and the Ministry of Health's Regional Health System for the geographic precinct which has oversight of the population health in the precinct.

The second engine refers to internal and external communication essential for mission alignment. A well-designed performance system communicates and engages your internal stakeholders — employees and volunteers. There is conceptual clarity in your organisational strategy, intended outcomes, and performance measures. A performance system should also be regularly communicated. When you communicate your performance, including areas for improvement to internal as well as external stakeholders, you are rallying support for your mission and purpose.

Organisations create value for shareholders when customers are willing to pay for the value proposition, which is defined as "the whole cluster of benefits the company promises to deliver" (Kotler & Keller, 2012). The logic is from the exchange of value between the company and the customer. This is the economic component of value.

However, in a NPO like a charity, beneficiaries or clients who are often taken to be the customer do not pay for the programmes or services or pay enough for the NPO to recover their operating costs. For the NPO, value proposition refers to the need the NPO aims to address, problems to solve, or benefits to bring to the community and its constituents.

Instead of appropriating value from beneficiaries, the NPO demonstrates their effectiveness to funders and donors to raise further financial capital to sustain their mission. It is therefore insufficient to focus only on the beneficiary's perspectives when communicating your organisation performance. Instead, NPOs must expand the focus to the perspectives of funders and donors, i.e., what is the value from their perspectives? For meals delivery, what is value in the eyes of AIC and the particular Regional Health System? How is this communicated to both stakeholder participants?

As another example, Project Bridge Vocational and Soft Skills Programme by YMCA of Singapore is an intervention to equip out-of-school and at-risk youths aged 15–21 with employable skills such as culinary and web design. The skills training would enable youths at-risk to be integrated and meaningfully engaged in society.[11] At the start of 2021, YMCA of Singapore, together with Tri-Sector Associates, launched a social impact guarantee model. Under the terms of agreement, the YMCA will return their donors' funds if they cannot achieve 75% placement into employment or education.

---

[11] *Source: The Business Times* (access: https://www.businesstimes.com.sg/life-culture/charity-offers-money-back-guarantee-for-youth-intervention-programme).

This placement target represents value or target return from the donors' perspectives.

A well-designed social performance system articulates its intended outcomes and incorporates the perspectives of other stakeholders. This is because social performance calls for many stakeholder participants who operate in a different sub-system, but their respective capability and capacity impact the achievement of the collective outcome.

Suppose job placement is the targeted outcome of the social impact guarantee model that funds the Programme by YMCA of Singapore. YMCA of Singapore leverages its organisational capabilities and capacities to train, support, and place youths in employment. The hiring of graduates into the employment market represents another sub-system's capability and capacity. Are there employers ready to absorb these graduates from the Programme into their payroll? Besides prospective employers, there is a slew of other factors that may influence job placements in the other sub-systems. These factors may range from individual youth's psychosocial issues (microsystem) and family circumstances (mesosystem) to the economic climate that affects job openings (exosystem). These extraneous factors in the ecosystem affect the achievement of outcomes for the intervention. Without engaging respective stakeholder participants and aligning each other's capability and capacity, the targeted outcome for youths at-risk may be threatened.

Akin to the expression "no man is an island", an organisation co-exists with others regardless of profit or non-profit.

Recall the non-profit ecosystem introduced in one of the earlier chapters. Given the interconnectedness and interdependence in the drive for social change, NPOs with a well-designed performance system must articulate and communicate their value proposition to different stakeholders in the ecosystem.

6.10   Performance Covenant

An effective performance system should enable you to produce and present the results your NPO is accountable to internal and external stakeholders. Accountability is not merely a legal responsibility and compliance requirement. Accountability is a moral imperative to donors, funders, taxpayers, beneficiaries, and volunteers, including supporters and advocates of your causes and the public.

I recall a debate I had in the boardroom during which I was adamant that the NPO does not poach key talents from our peer institutions. My rationale is simple. Unlike the commercial sector, I do not view them as competitors but partners and allies. The market for talent is much bigger than the sector in which the organisation operates. I appreciate the dissenting voices in the boardroom. That is the value of pluralism. What disturbed me was the argument that my perspective was weak in the absence of any written contractual agreement between us and our allies.

Moral duties transcend contractual obligations. There is a covenant between an NPO and the community. The covenant calls for the NPO to act and perform above what the law mandates. To me, this is the distinction between a mission-oriented organisation versus one that is profit-oriented.

A part of this covenant is the shift from leadership to stewardship of NPOs.

References

DeFina, L. F., Radford, N. B., Barlow, C. E., Willis, B. L., Leonard, D., Haskell, W. L., Farrell, S. W., Pavlovic, A., Abel, K., Berry, J. D., Khera, A., & Levine, B. D. (2019). Association of all-cause and cardiovascular mortality with high levels of physical activity and concurrent coronary artery calcification. *JAMA Cardiol, 4*(2), 174–181. https://doi.org/10.1001/jamacardio.2018.4628.

Diener, E. (2009). Assessing subjective well-being: Progress and opportunities. In: E. Diener (ed.), *Assessing Well-Being: The Collected Works of Ed Diener* (pp. 25–65). Springer Netherlands. https://doi.org/10.1007/978-90-481-2354-4_3.

Doran, C. M., & Kinchin, I. (2020). Economic and epidemiological impact of youth suicide in countries with the highest human development index. *PLoS One, 15*(5), e0232940. https://doi.org/10.1371/journal.pone.0232940.

Eagle, L., Dahl, S., Hill, S., Bird, S., Spotswood, F., & Tapp, A. (2013). *Social Marketing*. Pearson Education.

Ebrahim, A. (2019). *Measuring Social Change: Performance and Accountability in a Complex World*. Stanford University Press.

Ebrahim, A., & Rangan, V. K. (2014). What impact? A framework for measuring the scale and scope of social performance. *California Management Review*, 56(3), 118–141. https://doi.org/10.1525/cmr.2914.56.3.118.

Higueras-Fresnillo, S., Cabanas-Sanchez, V., Lopez-Garcia, E., Esteban-Cornejo, I., Banegas, J. R., Sadarangani, K. P., Rodriguez-Artalejo, F., & Martinez-Gomez, D. (2018). Physical activity and association between frailty and all-cause and cardiovascular mortality in older adults: Population-based prospective cohort study. *Journal of the American Geriatrics Society*, 66(11), 2097–2103. https://doi.org/10.1111/jgs.15542.

Kaplan, R. S. (2001). Strategic performance measurement and management in non-profit organisations. *Non-Profit Management and Leadership*, 11(3), 353–370.

Kaplan, R. S., & McMillan, D. (2020). Updating the balanced scorecard for triple bottom line strategies. Harvard Business School Accounting & Management Unit Working Paper (21-028).

Kaplan, R. S., & Norton, D. P. (1996). Linking the balanced scorecard to strategy. *California Management Review*, 39(1), 53–79.

Koba, S., Tanaka, H., Maruyama, C., Tada, N., Birou, S., Teramoto, T., & Sasaki, J. (2011). Physical activity in the Japan population: Association with blood lipid levels and effects in reducing cardiovascular and all-cause mortality. *Journal of Atherosclerosis and Thrombosis*, 18(10), 833–845. https://doi.org/10.5551/jat.8094.

Kotler, P., & Keller, K. L. (2012). *A Framework for Marketing Management* (5th edn.). Pearson Education.

Kwon, S., Lee, H. J., Han, K. D., Kim, D. H., Lee, S. P., Hwang, I. C., Yoon, Y., Park, J. B., Lee, H., Kwak, S., Yang, S., Cho, G. Y., Kim, Y. J., Kim, H. K., & Ommen, S. R. (2020). Association of physical activity with all-cause and cardiovascular mortality in 7666 adults with hypertrophic cardiomyopathy (HCM): More physical activity is better. *British Journal of Sports Medicine*, 55(18), 1034–1040. https://doi.org/10.1136/bjsports-2020-101987.

Lear, S. A., Hu, W., Rangarajan, S., Gasevic, D., Leong, D., Iqbal, R., Casanova, A., Swaminathan, S., Anjana, R. M., Kumar, R., Rosengren, A., Wei, L., Yang, W., Chuangshi, W., Huaxing, L., Nair, S., Diaz, R.,

Swidon, H., Gupta, R., Mohammadifard, N., Lopez-Jaramillo, P., Oguz, A., Zatonska, K., Seron, P., Avezum, A., Poirier, P., Teo, K., & Yusuf, S. (2017). The effect of physical activity on mortality and cardiovascular disease in 130 000 people from 17 high-income, middle-income, and low-income countries: The PURE study. *Lancet, 390*(10113), 2643–2654. https://doi.org/10.1016/S0140-6736(17)31634-3.

Lee, J. Y., Ryu, S., Cheong, E., & Sung, K. C. (2016). Association of physical activity and inflammation with all-cause, cardiovascular-related, and cancer-related mortality. *Mayo Clinic Proceedings, 91*(12), 1706–1716. https://doi.org/10.1016/j.mayocp.2016.08.003.

Nocon, M., Hiemann, T., Muller-Riemenschneider, F., Thalau, F., Roll, S., & Willich, S. N. (2008). Association of physical activity with all-cause and cardiovascular mortality: A systematic review and meta-analysis. *European Journal of Cardiovascular Prevention and Rehabilitation, 15*(3), 239–246. https://doi.org/10.1097/HJR.0b013e3282f55e09.

O'Donovan, G., Lee, I. M., Hamer, M., & Stamatakis, E. (2017). Association of "weekend warrior" and other leisure time physical activity patterns with risks for all-cause, cardiovascular disease, and cancer mortality. *JAMA Internal Medicine, 177*(3), 335–342. https://doi.org/10.1001/jamainternmed.2016.8014.

Sallis, J. F., Cervero, R. B., Ascher, W., Henderson, K. A., Kraft, M. K., & Kerr, J. (2006). An ecological approach to creating active living communities. *Annual Review of Public Health, 27*, 297–322.

Singer, P. (2015). *The Most Good You can Do: How Effective Altruism is Changing Ideas about Living Ethically*. Yale University Press.

Somers, A. B. (2005). Shaping the balanced scorecard for use in UK social enterprises. *Social Enterprise Journal, 1*(1), 43–56. https://doi.org/doi.org/10.1108/17508610580000706.

Trout, D. L. (1980). The role of social isolation in suicide. *Suicide Life Threat Behavior, 10*(1), 10–23. https://doi.org/10.1111/j.1943-278x.1980.tb00693.x.

Vijayakumar, L., Daly, C., Arafat, Y., & Arensman, E. (2020). Suicide prevention in the Southeast Asia region. *Crisis, 41*(Suppl 1), S21–S29. https://doi.org/10.1027/0227-5910/a000666.

Voracek, M. (2007). The nexus of suicide prevalence, helping behavior, pace of life, affluence, and intelligence: Contrary results from comparisons across nations and within the United States. *Perceptual and Motor Skills, 105*(3 Pt 2), 1119–1126. https://doi.org/10.2466/pms.105.4.

Zhao, H., Zhang, X. N., Shi, Z., Yin, L., Zhang, W. L., He, K., Xue, H. Q., Zhao, X. Y., & Shi, S. H. (2020). Association of level of leisure-time physical activity with risks of all-cause mortality and cardiovascular disease in an elderly Chinese population: A prospective cohort study. *Journal of Geriatric Cardiology*, *17*(10), 628–637. https://doi.org/10.11909/j.issn.1671-5411.2020.10.003.

Chapter 7

Using Systems Thinking for Organisation Transformation

7.1 Introduction

The final chapter of this book brings together the frameworks introduced in earlier chapters using systems thinking. The social change that most non-profit organisations (NPOs) aim to bring about is complex because of ambiguity, especially in social outcomes, too many stakeholders, and innumerable interdependencies. The complexity makes it crucial for NPOs to avoid a silo mentality and be part of an ecosystem involving multiple key actors.

We can apply system thinking theory to build collaborative partnerships and develop solutions where each actor can contribute its core capabilities and competencies for collective impact. NPOs can shape their narratives using story-telling techniques for stakeholder engagement and organisational transformation.

7.2 Definition of System and Systems Thinking

Donella Meadows (2008) defined a system as "an interconnected set of demands that is coherently organised in a way that achieves something or a purpose".

There is an ancient story of blind men and an elephant. A king brought a giant elephant to the city where the inhabitants were blind. The residents were curious to "see" the elephant. As they did not have any impression of the creature, they felt the elephant with their sense of touch. Each of them touched a different part of the elephant. Each thought they knew the elephant. The one who had touched the trunk shared that the elephant was like a water hose, long and

131

straight. The man who felt the legs and feet described the elephant as a pillar, sturdy and firm. Each felt one part out of the many. They each may be correct from their own perspective but did not describe the elephant wholly and adequately.

What is the moral of this story? We cannot know the system and its behaviour by learning the parts of the system or sub-system.

Could you relate to this story of the blind men and the elephant?

Do you recall the futile experience of your unilateral effort due to the constraint of other elements in the system?

Extending the blind men and elephant story: imagine that each blind man imagined the individual part and "over-developed" the part as the whole of the elephant. This imagined elephant would have an exceptionally long trunk, long ears or legs. It would look more like an "alien" than what we know as an elephant.

This story highlights the relevance of systems thinking in the NPO. Systems thinking helps us see the whole, the interconnectedness and the interactions within the NPO and externally with all the stakeholders. We can make sense of the complexity using systems thinking.

To better understand systems and interdependencies, we shall reference Chapter 2's "Five Cs" framework of the non-profit ecosystem. Exhibit 7.1 shows the Five Cs' Framework that includes the four Cs — Customer, Company, Collaborator, and Competitor. The four Cs represent a connected system, and together, they function like a system of systems — an ecosystem within the fifth "C", the Context of the sector.

An NPO comprises different departments to design, deliver, and allocate resources to the programmes and services. When a department works in a silo and optimises their part of work without interaction with other departments, programmes and services are delivered below the synergistic level to the primary beneficiaries. The organisation with any department that focuses narrowly on its performance would grow into the alien-looking elephant!

The well-meaning intention of the NPO may not be translated and delivered to its full extent through programmes and services with its internal departmental resources, and worst still, beneficiaries are impacted when internal coordination is sub-standard.

An option to avoiding this silo mentality is to explore collaboration with other organisations to complement each other's strengths and

Exhibit 7.1: Five Cs' Framework of Ecosystem in the Non-Profit Sector

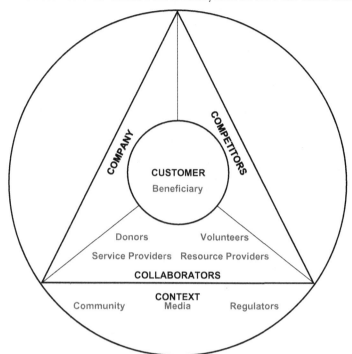

network. Win–win partnerships with collaborators could share or avoid costs while contributing to the vibrancy of the social ecosystem. Partnership and collaboration can be for marketing and communications, building talent pipelines, and even the sharing of physical office space.[1]

Zooming into the factor of *Customer* — the primary beneficiaries whom an NPO aims to serve in relation to its social cause and mission. Using the system lens to view customers allows us to see the wholeness of the individual — social, psychological, physiological, emotional, and cognitive dimensions and their social support system. To the individual, every dimension is interconnected. The problem is

---

[1] *Source*: *Forbes* (https://www.forbes.com/sites/forbesnonprofitcouncil/2018/03/07/12-effective-ways-to-operate-a-nonprofit-like-a-for-profit-business/?sh=130396134c6c).

usually multifaceted. This is why good intent delivered to fulfil only one aspect may not help to solve the problem.

For example, when we take care of persons with dementia, we have to consider the caregivers. Using the 5-Cs framework, the client is the *Customer*, the caregiver is the *Collaborator*, both the client and the caregiver are an integrated system. The client draws strength and comfort mainly from the caregiver. If the caregiver is burned out, the care of the client will be affected. Consequently, the client suffers when the support system collapses.[2] Engaging in conversations with the *Collaborator* — the caregiver — could illuminate issues with care and the burden they carry.

Mapping the ecosystem with 5 Cs is one way to understanding the interconnectedness and interactions to optimise system wide beyond a local siloed solution.

7.3 Analysing Root Causes through Systems Thinking

Systems thinking helps us to approach problems with a deeper and broader perspective. Reacting to symptoms with simplistic solutions is a common phenomenon. But symptoms are interrelated and manifestations of deeper root causes (Ng, 2005). Understanding the root causes allows us to appreciate more fundamental solutions to resolve the problem.

One approach is similar to Toyota's "5 whys" of questioning to go beyond the system level to uncover the root causes of the problem. Digging into the root causes allows us to identify the leverage points where minimum effort could achieve the optimum outcome.

For example, the questioning of whys has been used as part of a programme for rehabilitation at the Reformative Training Centre.[3] For ease of illustration, this example is based on linear causality. The purpose of the basic process is to facilitate the client to derive a causal map using the following steps:

> We give the clients an ambitious target, in this case — Successful Rehabilitation of Every Young Offender.

---

[2] *Source*: Channel NewsAsia (https://www.channelnewsasia.com/author/11666240).
[3] Contributed by Ms Christina Cheng — Singapore Director of Theory of Constraints for Education (TOCfE).

We ask them to come up with a list of constraints/obstacles that obstruct rehabilitation from being successful. (The clients love this part because everyone loves to complain and whine!)

We give them Post-it notes and ask each small group to choose one constraint, then start writing the causality (guided practice with examples first).

They then arrange the Post-it notes and connect them into a logic tree (causal map) to see the underlying core constraint or root cause. After identifying the core constraint or root cause, we will use another tool to unlock that constraint.

Exhibit 7.2 shows real examples of two groups of clients undergoing rehabilitation. The series of asking whys on reasons "the rehabilitation programme does not succeed" help to uncover the root cause. From Exhibit 7.2, we can see that the common root cause is the notion that "they want to feel good and avoid the problems they are facing." Placing the arrows from the bottom to the top, maps the issue to the root causes and helps the client to tell his/her stories. "I want to feel good and avoid the problems therefore I want to enjoy now. I want to enjoy now then I don't think about my future..." The process continues until it is connected to the issue, i.e., the unsuccessful rehabilitation programme.

Another example of identifying the root cause or the real needs of the community is to be immersed in the community of primary beneficiaries.

Dr Goh Wei Leong, who was the awarded *The Straits Times* Outstanding Singaporean of the Year in 2018, co-founded HealthServe in 2006. The award honours outstanding Singaporeans who have overcome great challenges to put our country on the world map or made it a better place through acts of selflessness.

HealthServe provides migrant workers with affordable healthcare, legal aid, social assistance, skills training, and free meals.[4]

Dr Goh and his friends opened a clinic in Geylang Lorong 23 with the intent to serve the migrant workers living there, charging only S$5 per consultation. While there was a ready pool of volunteer doctors keen to serve, the patient traffic remained dismal.

---

[4] *Source*: *The Straits Times* (https://www.straitstimes.com/singapore/doc-switched-from-maserati-to-charity-after-mongolia-trip).

Exhibit 7.2: Causal Maps of the Root Cause through Series of Why Questions

Rehab program does not succeed	Rehab program does not succeed
We don't see the need to change	We don't see the need to change
Lack of good & suitable courses	We feel 'famous' and 'recognised'
We don't give any feedback	We become boss in a negative way
We don't trust officers	Many youngsters follow us
Officers don't care about us	We boast & impress other youngsters
Officers look down on us	We feel proud of 'sucess'
We keep doing bad things	We have positive experience with illegal jobs
We are easily influenced by bad friends	We are easily influenced by bad friends
We don't think about our future	We don't think about our future
We want to enjoy now	We want to enjoy now
We want to feel good (not think about problems)	We want to feel good (not think about problems)

Simple process of asking and validating why

Eventually Dr Goh and his friends decided to cross the street to the even-numbered lanes in Geylang — a red-light district — where sex workers ply their trade and many migrant workers live right above the brothels.

"By crossing the street, we crossed over to the side of the vulnerable and oppressed," Dr Goh learnt that "… we had to move into the community." Soon, they made friends with a pimp, who introduced him to many of the migrant workers. And the migrant workers started coming to the clinic after Dr Goh and his friends spent many evenings to chatting and getting to know them.[5]

---

[5] *Source*: *The Straits Times* (https://www.straitstimes.com/singapore/charity-marks-10-years-of-offering-low-cost-medical-social-assistance-to-migrant-workers).

7.4 System Archetypes

Another valuable set of tools in system thinking is the system archetype (Kim & Anderson, 1998). Archetypes draw on past examples to examine and frame issues or problems that we presently face. While the system archetypes may not be exhaustive to match every situation we encounter, they provide us with a set of references and guide our assessment and development of practical and higher-leverage solutions (Ng, 2005).

One typical example is the "fixes that fail" archetype — identifying a problem symptom that resulted in a quick fix. Every time the quick fix is implemented, the symptoms go away for a while, and the unintended consequence is activated. The unintended consequence requires the quick fix loop to be faster with more attention and effort. As a result, the unintended consequences also increase, correspondingly.

A relatable example is the quick relief of a headache with a Panadol pill. The headache may go away for a while. When the headache returns, more of the painkiller is consumed. The unintended consequence or side effect over time is the over-reliance or addiction to painkillers. Instead of paying attention to discover the deeper underlying health issue, the quick fix resulted in a new problem. Exhibit 7.3 shows a simple causal loop of fixes that fail.

This "fixes that fail" archetype can also be applied in the people sector. With financial constraints, some charities allocate their available funding to programmes and interventions for clients, leaving little for capability building to enhance their efficiency and effectiveness in the long term. To complicate matters, donors are reluctant to fund overheads and expect 100% of donations to go towards beneficiaries or towards staff deployed directly for programmes and services.

Capability building, such as staff development, digitalisation efforts for data collection, and programme evaluation, is just as crucial for organisational sustainability. However, most of the funding is typically allocated to fund direct costs of programmes and services, even when there is more funding. The unintended consequence is an overload on the staff capacity, exacerbated by an increase in donor expectations for higher efficiency and effectiveness with more funding. Exhibit 7.4 shows another example of fixes that fails when there is a lack of capability building.

Exhibit 7.3: Simple Causal Loop of Fixes that Fail

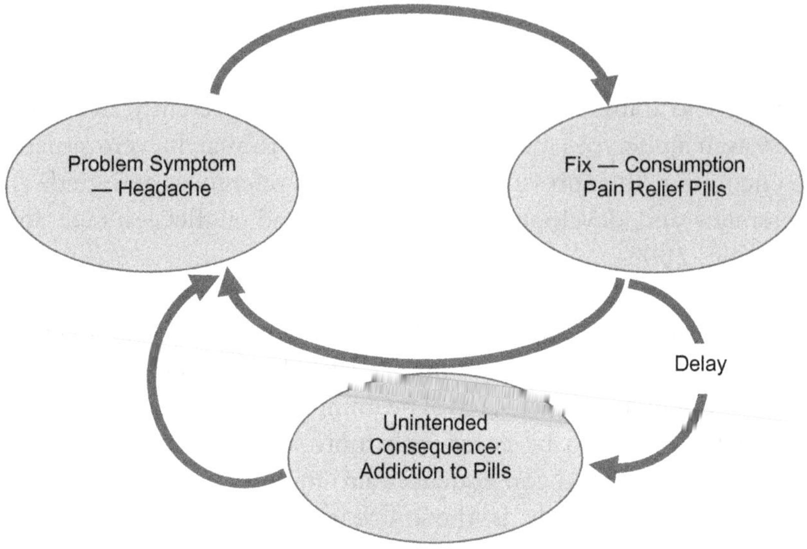

Finally, another cynical example is the case of toxic charity. Satisfying only the material needs of the poor and marginalised fixes only the symptoms. The unintended consequence is an increasing dependence on donors and volunteers.

To break the "fixes that fail" cycle, we have to acknowledge that the quick fixes are a mere short-term solution to alleviate the symptom while more time and effort go towards examining the root causes to solve the fundamental problem. Understanding systems thinking helps with problem-solving, and the system archetypes help us to appreciate dynamics in a system. The following are helpful resources to read up on system archetypes:

1. Systemic Board Governance: Creating Virtuous Cycles of Impact by Marty Jones (https://thesystemsthinker.com/systemic-board-governance-creating-virtuous-cycles-of-impact/).
2. Can Technology Transform the Non-Profit Sector by Suzaenne Laporte, Douglas Kelly, and Tosin Agbabiaka (https://insights.som.yale.edu/insights/can-technology-transform-the-nonprofit-sector).

Exhibit 7.4: Example of Fix that Fails Loop for NPO Focus on "Fixing — without Building Capability with Limited Resources"

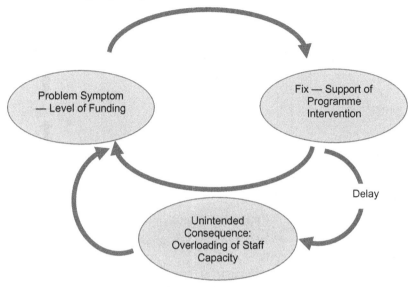

3. Kim, D. H., & Anderson, V. (1998). *Systems Archetype Basics.* Waltham, Mass, Pegasus Communications Inc.

7.5 Systems Thinking Framework

Leaders and managers are confronted with choices in their decision-making each day. How might one make the right decisions and choices? There are systems thinking frameworks that could guide our thinking. We will cover two in what follows, namely Hierarchy of Choices and Levels of Perspectives.

7.5.1 *Hierarchy of Choices Framework*

The hierarchy of choices framework provides a framework to guide us in our decision-making, achieve alignment and coherence in our thinking and actions. Exhibit 7.5 presents the hierarchy of choices framework.

In his book, *The Path of Least Resistance*, Fritz (1989) differentiates between the fundamental, primary, and secondary choices. He

Exhibit 7.5: Hierarchy of Choices Framework

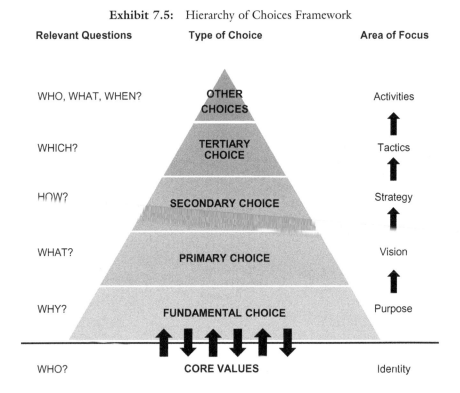

highlighted that it is difficult to choose one level if we do not have clarity of the option at the level below it.

Exhibit 7.5 shows the hierarchy of choices framework. As we look at the hierarchy of choices, as the NPO, we need to answer the questions:

- Who are we?
- What do we stand for?
- And what are our core values?

These questions address the identity of our organisation and guide our fundamental choice to answer the "Why?" and examine the purpose of the existence of our organisation.

Knowing the fundamental choice guides the development of the organisation's vision that will address the "What?"[6] When the strate-

---

[6] *Source*: The Systems Thinker (https://thesystemsthinker.com/leading-ethically-through-foresight/).

gic vision is compelling, vivid, and clear, people can devise the "Hows?" — strategies, tactics, and activities to move from current reality to the desired future (Kim, 2002).

7.5.1.1 *Hierarchy of choices at HCA Hospice Limited*

We shall use a local Institution of Public Character, HCA Hospice Limited (HCA) — Singapore's largest home hospice care provider and a registered charity since 1989, to illustrate the different choices taken and its alignment. HCA provides comfort and support to patients with life-limiting illnesses and life-threatening conditions regardless of age, religion, ethnicity, nationality, and financial status.

Exhibit 7.6 tabulates the hierarchy of choices: fundamental, primary, secondary, and tertiary, for HCA Hospice Limited. There is alignment and coherence of the choices made to strive towards HCA's vision of a centre of excellence for palliative care. The vision, purpose, and core values act as a compass and anchor the drive in the strategy, tactics, and activities.

It was clear that HCA's key strategy and value proposition is home palliative care. The value proposition is built on a no-charge strategy; patients admitted into their care are not charged for the professional services rendered. While one could argue that this no-charge strategy fully expresses one of HCA's core values of compassion, there is no publicly available information about the charity's long-term sustainability strategy. Perhaps communicating the rationale for the fundamental choice (i.e., no-charge strategy) given its impact on sustainability may rally more support from the public.[7]

During this COVID-19 situation, companies including NPOs also have to adapt to the situation to serve their beneficiaries. How does an NPO pivot using this hierarchy of choices framework?

Playeum is a small charity whose purpose is to allow children to use play and arts to experience the world. Playeum's vision is to be a beacon for families and children by creating a safe space to express themselves. Before COVID-19, Playeum's strategy was to design and deliver programmes for children and families.[8]

---

[7] Extracted from https://www.hca.org.sg.
[8] https://www.playeum.com/our-story.

Exhibit 7.6:   Hierarchy of Choices at HCA Hospice Limited

Activities	Day Hospice Care; Paediatric Palliative Care Services; Caregiver training; Bereavement Support and Outreach programmes and services
Tactics	24/7 Hotline; Psychological support to caregivers; Palliative training for caregivers
Strategy	Home palliative care at no charge to patient
Vision	To be a Centre of Excellence for Palliative Care
Purpose	Ensuring best quality of life for patients by delivering professional palliative care and compassion support to families. Nurturing the individuals who make our work possible and serve our community through continued training and development.
Identity	Compassion; Professionalism; Respect

Like many NPOs, Playeum was hard hit because of COVID-19. It saw a drastic drop in donations, the closure of its centre, and cessation of activities due to safe management measures.

Since children could not go to its centre, the executive director Charlotte Goh got her staff members and volunteers to partner with schools and charities to introduce its play curriculum. They also imparted skills by conducting workshops for the parents and teachers — staying true to the organisation's vision and purpose anchored on the value of play.[9]

The foundation of vision, purpose, and values guides and aligns the strategies, tactics, and activities in good times. In a crisis like the one caused by COVID-19, vision, purpose, and values act like a compass for NPOs to pivot their strategies, tactics, and activities amid chaos.

7.5.2 *Levels of Perspectives*

The levels of perspectives matrix facilitates discussion and thinking from events to systemic structure to mental models and vision. The leverage of problem-solving increases as we move up the levels of

---

[9] https://www.todayonline.com/commentary/trees-offer-leadership-lessons-non-profit-organisations.

perspectives. This matrix allows us to make sense of our experiences and for more effective problem-solving. Exhibit 7.7 shows the matrix for the levels of perspectives from events to vision, and at each level, it is mapped against current and future desired reality.

To diagnose the current reality, the following are guiding questions from events to vision levels (from bottom-up) to facilitate our systematic problem-solving:

- What are some specific events that characterise the current reality?
- Are those particular events indicative of a pattern over time?
- Are there systemic structures in place that are responsible for the pattern of behaviour?
- What mental models do we hold that lead us to put such structures in place? What are the prevailing assumptions, beliefs, and values that sustain those structures?

Exhibit 7.7: Levels of Perspectives

Level of Perspective	Current Reality	Desired Future Reality
Vision	What is the current vision-in-use?	What is the espoused vision of the future?
Mental Models	What are the prevailing assumptions, beliefs, and values that sustain the systemic structures?	What assumptions, beliefs, and values are needed to realise the vision?
Systemic Structures	Which systemic structures are producing the most dominant pattern of behaviour in the current system?	What kinds of systemic structures (either invented or redesigned) are required to operationalise the new mental models and achieve the vision?
Patterns	What is the behaviour over time of key indicators in the current system?	What is the current vision-in-use?
Events	What are some specific events that characterise the current reality?	What are some specific events that illustrate how the vision is operating on a day-to-day basis?

Increasing Leverage →

- What kind of vision are we operating out of that explains the mental models we hold? What is the current vision-in-use?

7.5.3 *Vision Deployment Matrix*

To develop our desired future reality, the following questions will guide us to achieving clarity in the visualisation from vision to events. This is also known as the Vision Deployment Matrix to develop our desired future reality.

- What is the espoused vision of the future?
- What mental models and the underlying assumptions, beliefs, and values will help realise the vision?
- What kinds of systemic structures are required to operationalise the new mental models and achieve that vision?
- What would be the behaviour over time and the critical indicators if the desired vision became a reality?
- What specific events would illustrate how the vision is operating on a day-to-day basis?

To illustrate the use of the levels of perspectives and vision deployment matrix, let me share a very inspiring story about the transformation of Xinmin Secondary School ("Xinmin") from its humble beginnings as an unknown neighbourhood school to its present status of an autonomous school. Exhibit 7.8 presents in detail the levels of perspectives and vision deployment matrix for Xinmin (Koh, 2002).

The lessons learnt from its transformation journey can be applied to charities and NPOs alike. The two key leaders leading the transformation in the 1990s were the Principals, Mr Goh Tong Pak (from 1992 to 1997) and Mr Lee Hak Boon (from 1998 to 2002).

Xinmin was founded by Mr Yap Fun Hong in 1945, who sold three piglets to rent three bungalows at Upper Serangoon Road to start the first school, known as Sin Ming High School, after World War II with the support of the local community. Mr Yap was the first principal of the School.

Interestingly, the guiding philosophy and educational policies were based on principles set forth by Sun Yat Sen. The goals were to

Exhibit 7.8: Levels of Perspectives of Xinmin Secondary School

Level of Perspective	Current Reality	Desired Future Reality
Vision	Every student can learn and succeed	• To be one of the best schools in Hougang in 5 years
Mental models	• Inward-looking • Self-reliance on internal resources	• Every student can learn and succeed • Outward-seeking • Community-based engagement for resources and support
Systemic structures	• No cut-off point for school • Students failed to indicate Xinmin as one of their choice schools • Established Government School status from 1984	• Leveraging on Alumni Network for resources & support • Red card system for student discipline management • Community look out for students loitering at arcades & prompt follow up with explanation & counselling • Self-study programme in the school with student support • Build conducive study environment • Staff development to build better teamwork

Patterns of behaviour	• Poor enrolment rate
	• High transfer out rate
	• High number of ill-disciplined cases
	• Poor public image
		• Ranking:
		  o From 134th in 1992 to 42nd in 1997
		• Enrolment rate (Students' Top 6 choices):
		  o From 951 (1992) to 3,481 (1997)
		• Enrolment rate (Students' first choice):
		  o From 32 (1992) to 644 (1997)
		• School achieved value-add Awards from 1992 to 1997
		• Eligibility of Secondary O level Students from 1992 to 1997:
		  o Junior College: 18.5% to 43.9%
		  o Pre-University/Polytechnic: 28.7% to 20.2%
		  o ITE: 38% to 28.9%
		  o Not Eligible: 14.8% to 7%
		  o GCE O Level 7–10 "O" passes (Express): From 17.9% (1992) to 45.9% (1997)

(Continued)

Exhibit 7.8: (*Continued*)

Level of Perspective	Current Reality	Desired Future Reality
		o GCE O Level 5–10 "O" passes (Normal): From 26.7% (1992) to 46.7% (1997)
Events	• Long queue of parents requesting for transfer to better secondary school. • Parent remarked, "even if Xinmin is the last secondary school in Singapore, I do not want my son to be here." • Xinmin was plagued with gangsters and fights. Children were led astray because of gang activities. • Truancy and unpunctuality rampant. • Average 15 absent cases per day. • Students felt embarrassed to admit that they are representing Xinmin Secondary when they were sent for Mathematics & Science competition in Junior College.	• Banner outside school — "You have made the right choice" to thank parents for giving the school a chance to educate their children. • Community Engagement — Mass run. • Self-study programme for study

enrich Singaporeans' lives, contribute to society's survival, develop the survival abilities of the people, and carry on the traditional lifestyle of the people. The fundamental tenets of the educational policies are: hands-on participation and leadership by example.

Xinmin was a private school then, and funding was raised through efforts of students, teachers, alumni, and the local community. The spirit of the School is: "I contribute to everyone's success, and everyone contributes to my success."

The School became a government school in 1984. At the end of 1987, the School which was running both primary and secondary levels was separated as Xinmin Primary and Xinmin Secondary Schools. Mr Goh Tong Pak, a student of the school in the 1950s, took over as the principal of Xinmin Secondary School in 1991.

The mental model was reframed from one that was inward-looking to outward-seeking for support of the whole community. This strategy led Goh to partner alumni, police force, residents, and neighbourhood businesses in rebuilding Xinmin. The partnership extended to the National Institute of Education (NIE) as a resource for good teachers and a concrete collaboration with primary schools to build pipelines of prospective secondary students.

Goh's vision for Xinmin, "To be one of the best schools in Hougang in 5 years." Communicating the shared vision and values at every opportunity.

Irrespective, Goh embraced the school's previous vision, which is, "Every student can learn and succeed", and this remained his belief and mental model. Goh led the school to reframe their thinking from "inward-focus" to "outward-seeking," exploring collaboration and community-based engagement for resources and support.

At the systemic level, when Xinmin was accorded the status of a government school, the school was not a popular choice among prospective students. None had indicated Xinmin as one of their secondary school choices then.

Externally, Goh leveraged the alumni networks for resources and funding support. Goh also collaborated with community partners and agencies like the police to curb disciplinary and public perception as Xinmin students were often loitering at arcades and shopping malls. Internally, to tighten the disciplinary standard, Goh established both "hard and soft" systems. Hard, with red card — warning and punishment system; Soft — with prompt follow-ups through explanation and counselling to change students' behaviour through a change of thinking and heart.

Goh viewed teamwork as critical to Xinmin's success and established staff development system to build teamwork. Goh also enhanced the school environment for more conducive study. With the systems established, from a poor public image, poor enrolment rate, high transfer-out rate, high number of student ill-disciplined cases, the new patterns of behaviour are:

• Ranking from 134th (1992) to 42nd (1997).
• Students who selected Xinmin as:
    o   One of Top six choices: From 951 (1992) to 3,481 (1997).
    ıı   First choice: From 32 (1992) to 644 (1997).

Under Goh's leadership, Xinmin also achieved consistent academic progress:

• Value-add awards from 1992 to 1997.
• Students' eligibility to progress JC increased from 18.5% (1992) to 43.9% (1997).
• GCE O Level 7–10 "O" passes (Express) improved from 17.9% (1992) to 45.9% (1997).
• GCE O Level 5–10 "O" passes (Normal) improved from 26.7% (1992) to 46.7% (1997).

At the events level, Goh implemented a self-study programme with student support to develop students' intrinsic motivation and conducted a mass run for community engagement. A banner was put up at the school entrance to thank parents for giving them a chance to educate their children. Contrast this with the long queue of parents requesting to transfer their children out of the school, cases of truancy, absenteeism, and students ashamed of representing Xinmin in external competitions.

In addition, Goh played a critical role to nurture his team. He treated every member as an essential valuable contributor to the organisational cause, listened and recognised the potential of every member. He created opportunities for interactions and social gatherings to build relationships at a personal level, not just professionally. He galvanised all the resources and talents, both internal and external, into a cohesive unit.

Goh led by example with honesty, integrity, and humility and earned the respect of his teachers, students, and the community around Xinmin. The people believed in Goh; they trusted his genuine desire to help others be successful and for the organisation's good. They believed that Goh was not in the making of a name for himself.

Through Xinmin's transformation, we can see how the levels of perspectives and vision deployment matrix could be applied for effective change management.

There is systems thinking behind the transformation:

- Mr Goh, the leader, set clear and realistic goals.
- Defined clear key indicators and metrics (linked to Chapter 6).
- Differentiated between short-term and long-term (immediate versus long-term outcomes in Chapter 6).
- Looked for consequences along multiple dimensions. (Root cause analysis versus quick fixes, engaged perspectives of different stakeholders in Chapter 4.)
- Committed to continuous learning, and this is observed from his emphasis on staff development (Chapter 5).

Goh, through his leadership and vision, had demonstrated how he led the organisation to overcome the four challenges of changes[10]:

- Why should we change?
- Why should we work together?
- What should we focus on?
- Why should we learn, unlearn, relearn?

7.6 Story-Telling for Social Change

"People are always blaming their circumstances for what they are. I don't believe in circumstances. The people who get on in this world are the people who get up and look for circumstances they want, and, if they can't find them, make them."

George Bernard Shaw (1856–1950)

---

[10] *Source*: The Systems Thinker (https://thesystemsthinker.com/from-event-thinking-to-systems-thinking/).

Stories can be a powerful engagement tool to solve an issue or communicate change. People can relate easily to stories based on their daily experiences and specific details about people and events. However, if the story-telling remains at the event level, the solutions developed will be largely reactive. To communicate the desired social change, we need to move beyond event-level story-telling to a deeper understanding of an issue and generalise insights to systemic perspectives and other situations.

We can use the above framework as a guide — applying the first two columns of the matrix of "current reality" and "desired future reality" to analyse the current situation and design an effective long-term solution, respectively.

For example, we can use the "current reality" column to understand the situation, take a "bottom-up approach", from events to vision levels. The "Events" level captures stories about specific incidents or events that indicate a problem. The next level, "Patterns over time," expands the larger patterns that unfold. Next, the "Systemic Structures" level looks at structures that resulted in the observed pattern of behaviour. Since those systemic structures are usually physical manifestations of deeply held mental models in the organisation, we can surface the mental models of the team and stakeholders involved in the systemic structure. Finally, at the "Vision" level, we explore the vision-in-use of the organisation that is influencing those mental models.

Analysing a problem or situation from these multiple levels forces us to go beyond usual event-level story-telling; while the details are rich, the ability to affect the future is low. Moving up the level of perspectives offers greater leverage for creating systemic change. This approach provides a framework to articulate the problem from multiple levels of perspectives.

To inspire the new vision for social change, we can use the "Desired Future Reality" column from a "Top-down" approach — from vision level to events level. Here, we articulate the desired vision and shared mental models with the stakeholders in order to drive the patterns of behaviour over time and events. This, also known as the Vision Deployment Matrix, provides a coherent framework to tell our story of a new espoused vision by connecting the contribution of stakeholders and expanding the details from vision to events levels.

This approach allows stakeholders to visualise their roles and contribution to the desired future reality at all levels.

The power of the belief that education is a ladder to help students and families move up their social status spurred Mr Goh Tong Pak despite the school's circumstances.

One of Xinmin alumni recalled Goh's declaration at one of the school assemblies, "Xinmin is my school. I do not care what others think of it. They may say there is no hope for its improvement or that it is a place of hopeless students; to me, you are not stupid. There is hope. Even if it means using my bare hands, I will make sure it improves... Let us strive for the better of Xinmin." The message expressed Mr Goh's passion and gratitude as an ex-student to serve the students and improve the school.

Goh communicated the school's vision with passion and unwavering belief at every opportunity, morning assemblies, staff meetings, and teacher contact time. His vision touched many teachers. Mr Goh also shared the plans, strategies, and target so that the followers know the organisation's direction and will be able to plan their own actions to help the organisation achieve its vision. Story-telling and metaphors are preferred to preaching and abstract concepts.

7.7 Conclusion

Patches of fabric are woven together with threads to create unique designs and textures of quilt. Metaphorically, our spirituality holds our lives together like how the thread holds together the layers of a quilt. Quilting is like a process in the search for meaning and purpose in life. Patches of fabric woven together are akin to the connection of human spirits, behaviours, and beliefs. Every human connection, like each piece of quilt, is distinctively designed.

Patchwork Quilt is a principle where leaders build partnerships with stakeholders to co-create solutions with them. This concept is a manifestation of system thinking that connects systems into a holistic whole to deliver a shared vision anchored on the deeper meaning, purpose, and common identity.

In her essay "Quilting and the Human Spirit", McMahon succinctly summarised this quilting process as the "threads of time" and "patches of life" connecting us with our past and giving meaning to our own lives.[11]

Leaders and managers in NPOs must think win–win and apply systems thinking to drive positive social change effectively.

References

Fritz, R. (1989). *The Path of Least Resistance: Learning to Become the Creative Force in Your Own Life*. Ballantine Books.

Kim, D. H., & Anderson, V. (1998). *Systems Archetype Basics*. Pegasus Communications Inc.

Kim, D. H. (2001). Leading ethically through foresight *Systems Thinker, 13*, 2–5.

Koh, W. (2002). *I Believe I Can Fly*. McGraw-Hill Education (Asia).

Meadows, D. (2008). *Thinking in Systems*. London: Earthscan.

Ng P. T. (2005). *The Learning School. Innovation and Enterprise*. Pearson Education South Asia.

---

[11] *Source*: The Baltimore Sun (https://www.baltimoresun.com/news/bs-xpm-1992-12-22-1992357024-story.html).

Appendix A
Tools to Promote Quality Conversations and Support Team Learning

A.1 What is Check-in/Check-out Process?[1]

The check-in process is a simple and effective tool to create a conducive environment for quality communication within a short time.

The check-in process is adopted from the Native American culture. The simple rules for their check-ins and check-outs (called "council rounds") include: be brief, and speak from the heart. It is an open invitation to participants to share what is on their minds.

The purpose of this process is to facilitate participants to share their concerns and issues openly, and to bring focus and complete presence to the subsequent meeting. It is akin to a physical warm-up before an exercise.

A.1.1 *How Do I Conduct a Check-in Process?*

Facilitate the participants to sit in a circle. Practice of deep and non-judgemental listening is an integral part of the check-in process. The leader can start before the meeting to pose a reflective question, "What is on my mind?"

The aim is to direct our focus to our thoughts and feelings. The leader extends an open invitation to whoever is ready to commence with the sharing of their thoughts. A time limit say one/two minutes for each speaker is set and the speaker will be presented with a talking object — be it a pen or a stick to symbolise authority to speak.

---

[1] https://thesystemsthinker.com/check-in-check-out-a-tool-for-real-conversations/.

Full attention is given to the speaker and the group will practise empathetic listening of the individual concerns and mental models. The benefit of the process, albeit for a short time, is that it creates a safer space to speak from our hearts and facilitates a deeper dialogue and conversation. When we acknowledge the concerns and speak our mind, it allows us to focus more effectively and to be fully present in the meeting. Through the process, it builds trust and enhances the quality of relationships among the team.

I practise this often during meetings, and I find this process very effective for all the voices of everyone in the room to be heard, especially those who are quiet and reserved, and it allows me to understand the state of minds of others.

A.1.2 *What is the Difference Between Check-in and Check-out Processes?*

The check-out is similar to the check-in process. The check-out process can bring closure to the meeting by asking a question that makes everyone reflect on their takeaways, learnings, or appreciation from the meeting.

A.2 After Action Review Process

An after-action review (AAR) is a collective reflection based on the practice from the US Army. AAR is a tool that leaders and managers of non-profit organisations can use to encourage team members to ascertain what happened, why it happened, and how to sustain strengths and improve on weaknesses after every task, activity, assignment, event, project, or programme. The tool maximises the learning benefits from each task (Darling & Parry, 2001).

A.2.1 *How Can We Do Collective Reflection with Our Colleagues?*

Similarly, we can frame these guiding questions for collective reflection for every task; before, during, and after our actions:

• What was expected to happen?
• What actually happened?
• What went well, and why?
• What did not go so well, and why?
• What can be improved, and how?

There are four steps for AAR: planning, preparation, conduct, and follow-up. Planning for dedicated time and space for the AAR session is essential. Preparation includes a safe and comfortable location, resources like flip chart and facilitator. Conduct of the AAR is guided by the facilitator with the guiding questions and active participation of the invitees. The facilitator guides the collective discussion and reflection through the process. The points raised and follow-ups are documented with clear accountability and monitoring purposes.

A.3 What is Open Space Technology?

One of the facilitation methods for open discussion and listening to the voice of the people is this idea of open space technology introduced by Harrison Owen.[2] Open Space Technology is useful for organisational retreat, conflict resolution, stakeholders, staff and community engagement, collaboration, and day-to-day meeting to learn about issues and perspectives.

Open Space Technology is a simple, yet powerful way to catalyse effective conversations to:

• Discuss complex issues in a short period of time.
• Enhance collaboration and inspires creative solutions.
• Listen to voices of passions, identify critical issues, and harness collective responsibility for solutions.

The open space concept anchors on autonomy and conversations in a psychologically safe space and time. The onus is on the people to turn up, participate, and leave at their choices. To create a powerful

---

[2] *Source*: OpenSpaceWorld.ORG (access: https://openspaceworld.org/wp2/what-is/).

event motivated by the passion and bounded by the responsibility of the participants, observe these four principles and one law:

- Whoever comes are the right people.
- Whatever happens is the only thing that could have happened.
- When it starts is the right time.
- When it is over, it is over.
- Law of Two Feet.

By the "Law of Two Feet", you are free to move to the discussion which you are most passionate and contribute to the issue.

A.3.1 *How Do I Organise an Open Space Event?*

The steps of organising an open space event are:

- Participants form in circles, each bears a basic theme to focus their efforts.
- Facilitator explains a few Open Space rules to guide the process.
- Participants of the circle are invited to identify any issue connected to the theme for which they have genuine interest and are ready to take some personal responsibility such as by convening a discussion group.
- Participants write their issues on pieces of Post-it (using one issue per post-it); announce the issues to the group and post the paper(s) on the wall. The wall will eventually be filled with issues and ideas for discussions.
- Issues are prioritised with ticks or votes from all participants.
- Groups are convened to discuss next steps, timelines, and identify individuals and groups to lead before the end of the event.
- The proceedings and discussions are recorded.

Harrison Owen's open space technology works best when conditions involve high level of complexity, diversity of people, presence of conflict, which means there is a real issue that people care about; and a sense of urgency for outcomes and actions to be taken. The crux is to create a psychologically safe space to tap onto the voices of the people involved organically from within. As participants learn to trust in the process, issues of importance will be discussed and prioritised with the next steps identified.

Reference

Darling, M. J., & Parry, C. S. (2001). After-action reviews: Linking reflection and planning in a learning practice. Reflections: The SoL Journal, 3(2), 64–72.

Appendix B
Mapping a Logic Model

In this exercise, you will map a logic model using the example of a frailty prevention programme called "Share a Pot" (www.shareapot.sg).

Physical frailty increases an elderly's risk of falls. One of the reasons for physical frailty is that our bodily functional reserves decline with ageing (Lee *et al.*, 2020; Lim *et al.*, 2017). Physical frailty can be measured by a clinical frailty score from 1 for "very fit" to 9 for "terminally ill". Increased clinical frailty is associated with adverse health outcomes like higher falls risks, extended stay in institutional care, increased comorbidity, and commonality risks.

"Share a Pot" aims to prevent and manage frailty of community-dwelling seniors using physical activity and nutritional intake. A reduction in physical frailty among community-dwelling seniors can lower the risk of falls. Falls impact a senior's mobility and quality of life, and likely increases healthcare costs for the senior.

As the name suggests, the central idea of this project is the sharing of a pot of nutritious soup. A typical programme agenda for this project begins with a low impact physical fitness activity for seniors designed and led by a physiotherapist. Thereafter, the seniors stay behind to enjoy a bowl of hot soup and catch up with friends. The activity that follows is the monitoring of their gait, grip, and balance to assess any falls risks among them by a therapist, community nurse or any one of the seniors who is her/himself trained to administer the measurement.

Using the programme information above, map the logic model for "Share a Pot" by stating the intervention and adding the components into each column of the logic model. You may use the following template as a reference.

References

Lee, S. Y., Kua, H. A., Qiu, W., Lai, K. Y., Jumala, J., Yong, L., Tay, E. L., Mah, S. M., & Lim, W. S. (2020). Exercise as medicine in frailty prevention and management: Why now, why here, and making it happen. *Annals of the Academy of Medicine, 49*(10), 810–813. https://doi.org/10.47102/annals-acadmedsg.2020158.

Lim, W. S., Wong, S. F., Leong, I., Choo, P., & Pang, W. S. (2017). Forging a frailty-ready healthcare system to meet population ageing. *International Journal of Environmental Research and Public Health, 14*(12). https://doi.org/10.3390/ijerph14121448.

INTERVENTION [State the intervention]					
Internal			External		
Inputs	Activities	Outputs	Individual outcomes	Community outcomes	Social impact

[Map the components in each column]

Appendix C

Performance Reporting: Examples and Resources for Quantitative and Qualitative Methods

Methods	What is it?	How is it used?	Resource link
Quantitative: Expected Return and Cost-Effectiveness	An example of expected return and cost-effectiveness is Social return on investment (SROI), which measures social, environmental, and economic outcomes and uses monetary values to represent them. SROI can be conducted retrospectively based on actual outcomes, also known as evaluative or forecast, i.e., measured by predicting social value creation if intended outcomes are achieved.	SROI can be used as a tool for strategic planning, communicating impact, attracting funding for projects, or making project decisions. It supports strategic discussions by helping stakeholders understand and maximise the social value an activity creates. SROI is an important tool for identifying common ground between an organisation and its stakeholders, helping to maximise social value.	https://socialvalueuk.org/wp-content/uploads/2016/03/The%20Guide%20to%20Social%20Return%20on%20Investment%20 2015.pdf.
	The benefit–cost ratio quantifies the social good of a project or programme relative to its cost, providing a basis to compare the performance of one project against another.	It determines if the project or programme achieves its intended purpose and objectives and ascertains, if — and by how much — its benefits outweigh its costs. Provides a basis for	https://www.aisp.upenn.edu/wp-content/uploads/2015/09/0033_12_SP2_Benefit_Cost_000. pdf. https://www.robinhood.org/what-we-do/metrics/.

The economic rate of return provides a suitable metric, derived from a cost–benefit analysis that compares the economic costs and benefits of a programme. In the cost–benefit analysis by the Millennium Challenge Corporation (MCC), the costs of a project include all required economic costs of all involved parties, as well as opportunity costs associated with the non-financial resources utilised.	comparing decisions, comparing the total expected cost of each option with its total expected benefits, thereby improving decision-making and leading to more efficient outcomes. It is a micro-economic growth analysis that captures the expected increases in local incomes through environmental and social improvements. An example is the effect of clean water on health outcomes for improved female educational attainment on incomes.	https://www.mcc.gov/our-impact/err.

(Continued)

(*Continued*)

Methods	What is it?	How is it used?	Resource link
	Subjective well-being (SWB) is the scientific term for happiness and life satisfaction primarily assessed by self-report surveys and other concurrent measures like personality, contextual influencers, and reports by family, friends, and colleagues.	Research has indicated that people high in SWB are healthier and function more effectively compared to people who are angry, depressed, or stressed.	https://nobaproject.com/modules/happiness-the-science-of-subjective-well-being#content.
Systematic Reviews	Systematic review sums up the best available research on a specific issue or question by synthesising the results of many studies. An example is Campbell review, which uses rigorous methods including, a meta-analysis of research evidence and theory-based analysis of qualitative evidence.	Systematic review shows areas with strong, weak, or non-existent research on the effect of interventions or initiatives. By demonstrating where knowledge is lacking, it can be a useful guide for future research.	https://www.campbellcollaboration.org/. https://www.ncbi.nlm.nih.gov/pmc/articles/PMC3894019/.

	To avoid bias, a Campbell review includes a search for unpublished work, is typically international in scope, and undergoes peer review and editorial review.		https://www.echocommunity.org/resources/53f99bb6-f532-4606-8229-0327c16dbd3c.
Qualitative: Participatory and Relationship-Based Methods	Participatory survey solicits performance feedback from constituents or stakeholder participants to benchmark against peers. Instead of using preset indicators, it relies on field-level stories of change and draws out knowledge of local people for planning interventions. Examples of the methods and tools include Rapid Rural Appraisal, Mobility map, Social map, and Transect.	The use of participatory survey and planning methods in the development process facilitates information flow between the community and the development organisation and encourages community ownership of projects, thereby enhancing accountability.	

(*Continued*)

(Continued)

Methods	What is it?	How is it used?	Resource link
	Most significant change is a qualitative and participatory monitoring and evaluation technique which does not involve quantitative indicators and is instead based on the collection and systematic selection of field level stories of reported changes from development activities.	It facilitates project and programme improvement by focusing work towards fully shared visions and explicitly valued directions and uncovering valuable outcomes not initially identified.	https://www.adb.org/sites/default/files/publication/27613/most-significant-change.pdf.
	Human interest stories document the experiences of individuals who are affected by projects run by private voluntary organisations, emphasising the human aspect and personalising the project's successes and challenges. They can take the form of either a success story or a learning story.	Human interest stories are used to complement measurement and evaluation data by providing an individual's perspective of a project. They can also help raise awareness on issues through media campaigns and respond to reporting needs of donors or funders.	https://fr.fsnnetwork.org/sites/default/files/memodule_humaninterest.pdf.

Participatory evaluation is an evaluation process that provides for active involvement of all relevant stakeholders, including partners and beneficiaries, throughout all phases right from planning, data gathering, and analysis to identifying evaluation findings and conclusions and preparing performance improvement plan.	Participatory evaluations improve programme performance by providing a framework for listening and learning from programme beneficiaries, field staff, and other stakeholders. Involving insiders in identifying evaluation questions, gathering, and analysing data also increases the likelihood of the information being used to improve performance.	https://pdf.usaid.gov/pdf_docs/Pnadw101.pdf.
Focus group interview is a low-cost quick appraisal technique that provides qualitative information on the performance of development activities. It involves a facilitator guiding a group of people in a discussion on their experiences, feelings, and preferences about a topic,	Focus group interviews can be useful in all phases of development activities — planning, implementation, monitoring, and evaluation to soliciting insights, and recommendations of programme staff, clients, or beneficiaries, technical experts, and other stakeholders.	https://www.eiu.edu/ihec/Krueger-FocusGroupInterviews.pdf. https://www.ndi.org/sites/default/files/USAID%20Guide_Conducting%20Focus%20Groups.pdf.

(Continued)

(Continued)

Methods	What is it?	How is it used?	Resource link
	using probing techniques to solicit views and ideas. Its group setting provides checks and balances, minimising false or extreme views, though its flexible format can make it prone to facilitator bias.		
	Projective techniques are a subset of personality testing in which the examinee is given a simple unstructured task, with the goal of uncovering personality characteristics. Despite their wide prevalence and application, projective techniques are quite controversial.	Projective techniques can be used in an evaluation to provide a prompt for interviews. An example is photo language where participants select one or two pictures from a set and use them to illustrate their comments about a topic.	https://www.betterevaluation.org/en/evaluation-options/projective_techniques.
	Key informant interview is a qualitative in-depth interview typically conducted	Key informant interviews are useful to get information on pressing issues in the	https://healthpolicy.ucla.edu/programs/health-data/trainings/Documents/tw_cba23.pdf.

over telephone or face-to-face with community leaders, professionals, or residents who have hands-on knowledge of problems in the community and can give recommendations for solutions. | community from people with diverse backgrounds and opinions. Individual and small group discussions can be particularly useful to create a safe setting for a frank discussion on sensitive topics. |

Qualitative: Integrative Approaches — Strategic Learning, Planning and Evaluation, and Collective Impact	Strategic Learning and Evaluation link performance measurement to strategy by methods such as formative and developmental evaluation, balanced scorecards, strategy maps, and dashboards.	Strategic Learning and Evaluation help an organisation understand the progress and impact of funding and provide a framework for increasing effectiveness.	https://www.fsg.org/areas-of-focus/strategic-learning-evaluation.
	Social enterprise balanced scorecard is a performance measurement tool that uses a strategy map to connect an organisation's day-to-day processes to its organisational	It can help bring transparency to the decision-making framework, capturing benefits and consequences and ensuring that social enterprise managers make decisions	https://www.open.edu/openlearn/money-business/sustainable-innovations-enterprises/content-section-3.2.4.

(*Continued*)

(Continued)

Methods	What is it?	How is it used?	Resource link
	goals. Instead of focusing on how an organisation currently operates, it is concerned with creating a strategy to drive future direction.	driven by strategy instead of short-term imperatives.	
	Though originally designed for a holistic diagnosis of business performance, the balanced scorecard can be amended for social enterprises.		https://ink.library.smu.edu.sg/cgi/viewcontent.cgi?article=1010&context=lien_research.
	Constellation mapping is a way to bring together multiple groups or sectors to work towards a joint outcome. Constellations of small self-organising teams handle social change activities such as public education, service delivery, or	The emphasis on action teams accommodates conflicting priorities of disparate groups. Since constellations flow from opportunism instead of rigid plans, interests, and needs of each group can be balanced within the goal of productive collaboration.	https://www.collectivetransitions.com/codesign-platform.

research. These teams in turn thread into an overall partnership, which is held together with a framework that shares leadership between the partners.

Collective Impact initiatives involve multiple activities, programmes, and initiatives, all of which operate in mutually reinforcing ways.
By building common agenda and shared measures of success, Collective Impact helps bring together organisations across sectors to solve social problems.

Though not a solution for all partnership needs, the constellation model is helpful for organisations that want to solve concrete problems within the context of a rapidly changing, complex ecosystem.

Collective Impact helps non-profits coordinate agendas with other partner organisations to reinforce activities, communicate with collaborators, and collect and analyse data for shared measurement. It also helps funders focus on the broader issue instead of individual grantees and think about the long-term processes and gradual impact instead of short-term solutions.

https://collectiveimpactforum.org/sites/default/files/Learning_in_Action_Evaluating_Collective_Impact.pdf.

https://www.fsg.org/sites/default/files/tools-and-resources/Collective_Impact_Webinar_presentation.pdf.

(*Continued*)

(Continued)

Methods	What is it?	How is it used?	Resource link
	Performance dashboard similar to the dashboard in a car, a non-profit dashboard gives important information to key decision-makers in a quick-read way. Action lights (that help focus on specific actions) and trends (showing improvement or decline over time) can be particularly useful additions to dashboards.	In contrast to complex financial presentations, dashboards can help focus decision-makers on areas needing attention. Reporting metrics on programme implementation, compliance and risk management, and fundraising can be particularly useful aids for decision-making.	ttps://blueavocado.org/board-of-directors/a-nonprofit-dashboard-and-signal-light-for-boards/.

Index

collective intelligence, 85
Commissioner of Charities (COC), 22, 30
common good, 15, 17
common social good, 16
common language, 2, 3, 62
communication, 3, 20, 33, 39, 56, 61, 69–71, 75, 86, 119, 120, 122, 123
Communities of Practice (CoP), 93
community and social services, 20
community-dwelling seniors, 27, 110
community engagement, 13, 148
community outcomes, 19, 119
company, 5, 7, 13, 22, 24–26, 33, 37, 47, 124, 132
competitors, 24, 28, 29, 36, 47, 126, 132
complementary organisations, 29, 33, 113
complex system, 18
constraints, 31, 37, 42, 50, 77, 94, 123, 132, 135, 137
core constraint, 135
context, 2, 6, 10, 24–27, 30, 33, 36, 39, 55, 56, 76, 80, 105, 107, 115, 132, 133
continuous learning, 93, 123, 148
contribution, 9, 30, 115, 150
conversational guidelines, 87
cooperatives, 20, 21
core competencies, 47, 49, 94
core theory of success, 85
corporate social responsibility, 37
covenant, 126
performance covenant, 125
current reality, 141, 143–146, 150

customer, 2, 6, 7, 13, 14, 24–26, 32, 33, 61, 111, 112, 124, 132–134
customer satisfaction, 13

data collection, 121, 137
data governance framework, 122
deadweight, 122
deep learning, 77
desired future reality, 143–146, 150, 151
desired social change, 10, 16, 17, 99, 107, 115 117, 150
digitalisation, 4, 78, 79, 137
digitalisation processes, 79
digital transformation, 4, 32, 78, 79
digitisation, 4, 45, 78
displacement, 122
diverse perspectives, 77
donor, 5, 9, 14, 16, 25–29, 32, 33, 39, 51, 56, 57, 60, 61, 63, 67, 84, 85, 112, 113, 117, 120, 124–126, 133, 137, 138
double-loop learning, 89–91
downstream, 60, 61, 106, 107
dual bottom-line, 7
dynamic complexity, 10

economic rate of return, 117
ecosystem, 13
ecosystem strategy map, 111, 113, 114
non-profit ecosystem, 13
simple ecosystem, 19
effective altruism, 117
embrace creativity, 76, 77
emergent learning, 74

web analytics, 33
wholeness of the individual, 133
wicked problems, 20
win–win partnerships, 133
workplace learning, 75, 93, 94, 95
World Health Organization
  (WHO), 106

Xinmin Secondary School,
  144–149, 151

YMCA of Singapore, 124, 125
Yong, Danny, 15

Printed in the United States
by Baker & Taylor Publisher Services